SLEEPING WITH THE BISHOP

2/4/23
For Gwendolyn Brown,
Thank you for your
support and presence.
Trena

TRENA TURNER

MINDSTIR MEDIA

Sleeping With The Bishop
Copyright © 2022 by Trena Turner. All rights reserved.

No part of this book may be used or reproduced in any manner whatsoever without written permission, except in the case of brief quotations embodied in critical articles and reviews. For more information, e-mail all inquiries to info@mindstirmedia.com.

Published by Mindstir Media, LLC
45 Lafayette Rd | Suite 181| North Hampton, NH 03862 | USA
1.800.767.0531 | www.mindstirmedia.com

Printed in the United States of America
ISBN: 978-1-958729-25-0

I dedicate this book to my mom, Mother Mary Ann George for a lifetime of support and for cultivating in me a love for reading, writing and storytelling.

I honor and thank God for my husband, Bishop Rufus K. Turner. Your integrity and amazing faith in God has inspired my growth and determination to serve the kingdom in excellence. I am blessed to experience ministry with you, you make it adventurous and fun. I am thankful for the joy and laughter brought to my life by our children; Jbar, Tia, JJ and our grandchildren; Janae, Dajon, Micah, Emani, Xavier, Jaelynn and Joey. You all make my heart smile.

For my siblings, Cheryl, Deryl, Errol, and Wilma thank you for your unwavering love and for allowing me to lead from the rear (youngest).

I thank the Victory In Praise Church staff and members who have allowed me to freely share my gifts; you have encouraged me to completion, since my first shared vision for this work.

To my Yayas, Penni and Vicki, I am humbled and amazed by your willingness to consistently display love in action.

I honor Father God for equipping and using me, in spite of me, in His kingdom. I thank Him for placing within me the exact elements needed to live life in a way, that I hope, brings glory to His name.

To the lives and memories of my mother-in-love, Mother Olean C. Turner, brother Herman Lee George, Jr., son J'barrie K. Turner, and grandson Joseph Barnes, IV.

To the lives and memories of my father, Herman Lee George, mother-in-love, Mother Olean C. Turner, brother Herman Lee George, Jr., son J'barrie K. Turner, and grandson Joseph Barnes, IV.

CONTENTS

Foreword vii

Confession ix

Chapter 1   God Kept Me (For Such A Time As This) 1

Chapter 2   Pillow Talk. 7

Chapter 3   Jehovah Wake-Him-Up. 14

Chapter 4   Enemies Camp 18

Chapter 5   Things That Go Bump In The Night. 23

Chapter 6   Miss Ministry. 29

Chapter 7   It Adds No Sorrow 34

Chapter 8   No More Church 39

Chapter 9   Church Hurt 44

Chapter 10 Faith Versus Common Sense 54

Chapter 11 Lest We Offend. 60

Chapter 12 Drained. 67

Chapter 13	Sometimes Giants Look Like Ants	.74
Chapter 14	In Just A Few Hours	.83
Chapter 15	God's Word Stands	.88
Chapter 16	My Hope Is Built On Nothing Less	.92
Chapter 17	Attacks	.97
Chapter 18	I Get To Worship	104
Chapter 19	Dangers Seen And Unseen	109
Chapter 20	Taking God's Breath For Granted	115
Chapter 21	Peace Must Be Chosen	125
Chapter 22	What We Do With It?	131

Sleeping With The Bishop 135

FOREWORD
BY BISHOP RUFUS K. TURNER
Founder of Victory In Praise Church Stockton
& author of the book A Shepherd's View

Believe it or not, I met Trena soon after she was born! We grew up together in the same church. It was never part of our initial thought and it was not our parent's plan, but it was the providence of God, for us to grow up together; marry, have children, go to college, while establishing a church and a social justice ministry. You talk about a ride-or-die couple.

In many of the pre-marital counseling sessions we've had the privilege of conducting, Trena and I inform couples that they will be the best witnesses of each other's personal lives as they journey through life together. It has been just that for us. We're on the verge of celebrating 44 years of marriage as I write these words. And we are still going strong.

The personal and insightful stories you are about to encounter will provide you with a glimpse into the behind the scene life and personality of a very wise and articulate woman. Each chapter is designed to provoke deep thought and reflection. Instead of WWJD (What would Jesus do?), reflect on WWYD (What would you do?) in each situation. Trena has a way with words that is uniquely hers. She will say something that will leave you speechless and will later have you saying within yourself, "Wait a minute. Did she just tell me off?"

Trena has mentored many in the corporate world as well as within the Christian community. Some chapters will reveal a glimpse into her serious side, while others will provide you comic relief. Don't be afraid to shed a few tears as you journey with her through many of her life's ups and downs. Everyone has an image of what it is like to be married to a pastor or a bishop. Looking from a distance you may see one thing, but prepare yourselves, are you ready to go behind the scenes?

I hope you're ready for the journey,
BishopT

CONFESSION

Confession is indeed good for the soul. So, to get it out of the way I'll make my confession right up front before I lose the courage to state it. But what exactly does 'confession' entail? Confession is an acknowledgment, a declaration, an assertion, or an admission. On second thought, perhaps before I seal my fate and no doubt call down judgment upon myself, I'll take some time remembering how I got here.

Believe it or not, it was never my intention to be where I am today. It was not a life-long dream or desire. I did not plan it, pray for it, nor did I in any way cause it to happen. The more I think about it, I am more and more convinced I am simply a pawn in some master plan that was written and designed long ago. I was chosen to fulfill this role that many would shy away from and perhaps, even more, would kill for.

I was just a teenager when this plan began to unfold. I didn't know it at the time but many, many people were instrumental in ensuring that I was properly prepared to take the rap for my current situation. It must have required unimaginable amounts of planning, patience, prodding, protection, pruning, pressure, and prayer to ensure that I was strategically set on the proper path to meet my destiny.

Destiny: that is exactly what I feel occurred. I feel I personally met up with destiny. The problem with destiny is that it is often larger than what you feel you can adequately manage. You feel unworthy, unprepared, and positive that there is someone out there that would have been the better selection to fill the required role … at least initially. Furthermore, destiny often eludes an individual because they have not invested the required time or allowed themselves to be molded and shaped to make certain that at the appointed time, they are in the precise place required to meet their destiny.

Not to seem pompous or proud, I do not believe anyone truly meets their destiny on their own. It requires each individual to allow others to push them along as needed. We learn from others' experiences and allow those we trust, our mentors, teachers, coaches, and elders, to peer into our very souls and spy out the potential buried within us. Then they must be willing to assist in the process of excavating the elusive potential, bringing the hidden treasure to the surface.

After all the encouragement of others along the way, however, only you are accountable for your accomplishments and actions. Therefore, when it's time for confession, you aren't confessing what someone else did or didn't do. Your confession has to be what you took part in. The action that I have been part of did not just take place. It was not a one-time incident or occurrence. I am a repeat and long-time offender. I have had challenges in this role but have determined that I am the right one to continue in this position.

I chose not to spend any time talking about the other individual involved. Many have heard from the 'other' perspective. I now want to tell my story, from my perspective. God had a plan for me before I was ever born. Beyond being support and help to my husband, God created me and placed me in a unique position to carry out His plans for my life. I have been without a voice for some time, and I do have a story to tell. Many of you play major roles in my story. You had to have known it. Up front or behind the scenes, I play a significant role in your lives as well. Who am I? What is my role? Well … I am sleeping with the Bishop, and oh yes, I have his ear!

[Bishop - a senior member of Christian clergy with spiritual authority over other pastors or clergy.]

> *"I chose you before I formed you in the womb; I set you apart before you were born. I appointed you a prophet to the nations."*
>
> Jeremiah 1:5 HCSB

CHAPTER 1

GOD KEPT ME (FOR SUCH A TIME AS THIS)

What a truly awesome life this is! I could not have imagined in a million-trillion years what God had in store for me. I have been blessed beyond measure. It is simply amazing that with all that God has entrusted me with; with the awesome man of God that He has blessed me with, my life started out as one of mediocrity and commonplace; sprinkled with just the right amounts of pain and laughter, loss and love, that gives a depth of character.

I grew up the youngest of four stair-stepped children. I had one sister and two brothers, and our dad and mom raised us in a modest three-bedroom home in a nice neighborhood. Except for the fact that we were not in rural America or white, we could easily have been the Waltons, the family from Leave It To Beaver, or any other stereotypical unassuming family unit. God gave me a childhood friend that has weathered many storms in life with me and grew to become my second sister.

God planted me in a place of safety. In my adolescence, I had a mother who loved and cared for me, a father who absolutely adored his children, and in my opinion, I was his favorite. My father was a police officer in Hunter's Point for the city of San Francisco. My mom was a stay-at-home mom so we reaped the benefits of home-prepared lunches and hot-cooked meals. After school, we returned home to a household with adult supervision. My father played the piano and accordion, so we occasionally sang together as a family, had regular game times, and we all sat down for mealtimes together. Our family took vacations across the country together, and to this day I have fond memories of a happy childhood. It would be many years before I learned that much of the love and happiness felt was what only a child could and should know. There were things brewing beneath the surface that my parents kept the lid on to protect and shelter their little ones.

An attempted kidnapping of my sister, sugar poured into our family vehicle's gas tank, and visits to the city with our dad where we (the children) had to sit outside in the car for unspecified time periods, were all great adventures, in the mind of a child. And later, the dotted lines to ominous occurrences in our lives were never definitively drawn but were loosely intimated. In November of 1967, my father was shot twelve times, at the police office, where he was stationed in Hunter's Point, with a .30 caliber rifle. He fought to live but succumbed to his wounds in December, a month later. This tragic incident left my mother a widow of four, at a young 31 years of age.

Life shifted after the loss of our father. Because of the grace of God and the determination of my mom, even with the enormity of impact on her incredibly young life, things, for us, did not radically change. Most children believe their mother to be pretty, but my mom actually was. I recall a few men that would attempt to catch her attention or would show up with flowers to win her over. They were all wasting their time. Mom refused to remarry or even date. She later explained that, in her mind, there was too great a risk of having any man in the house, around her daughters. She would protect her family at all costs. Mom said there were some things that she would have to kill someone and go to jail for.

After Herman's death, (we all called him Herman because he said he was too young and good-looking to have four children), Mom did not return to the workforce but instead chose to make her 'fixed income' work and stay home to single-handedly raise her four children - all under the age of eleven. Looking back, I can recall many times, while the four of us were eating and wanting second helpings, mom would say, to no one in particular, that she would eat later or that she wasn't hungry. Of course, we later realized that often there was not enough food for four hungry children and her to eat, so Mom would skip many meals to allow her babies to eat their fill. In Mom's mind, it was all worth it to be able to stay home, nurture, and watch her children grow. Grow we did. As children will, we all took different paths in life. Some got jobs directly, some went on to college first, we all married, some stayed married, and some re-married. The girls eventually chose Christ and served in ministry, and the boys are still finding their way.

Despite every heartache and joyful life experience, my life felt very ordinary. Yet, when I look back over my life, I see the hand of God at every stage in my life. I see that God was there teaching me the importance of family and hierarchy in the family. God taught me, through the examples and actions (or non-actions) of my mother, that you don't have to act on everything you think you know. And, that prayer absolutely changes things. Mom taught me, through observation, that we are all much stronger than we think we are, and we can endure much more than we would ever choose to if asked. God let me experience the pain of loss that seemed almost unbearable to a seven-year-old, and yet see that tomorrow still comes and life will go on, altered but not 'un-doable.' God kept my mom, my family, and me from sinking into total despair.

I see God's hand, in my early teens, as I tried to experiment with drugs, but He never let me enjoy the experience or quite fit in. With every attempt, God kept the high from having an impact. God blocked any pleasure or enjoyment so that the temptation to continue eventually waned and then ceased. I see God's hand and protection, during my high school years when the enemy wanted me to be killed by an agitated and inexperienced police officer. As I looked down the barrel of his shotgun, God gave the officer the presence of mind to not pull the trigger. Immediately afterward, my friends and I saw the shaken officers at the bottom of the hill sitting dazed in their patrol car. God knows how close they came to ending our lives and altering theirs forever. I can only imagine how close by viewing the fear on their faces as they leaned out of their patrol car. God kept me.

I see God there, blocking the plans of the enemy over and over, as I tried to give away my virginity before marriage. Every scheme was spoiled, and I walked down the aisle of matrimony, in purity at seventeen years of age. God was there, as I engaged in sex outside of my marriage, yet God kept away sickness, disease, and pregnancies outside of wedlock. Where the enemy thought he could hold this over me to use at the appropriate time to destroy our marriage, God lovingly pressed upon me to confess to my husband, not because I was caught or found out, but because I had sinned and was in need of his forgiveness and in need of God's restoration.

God was right there as the enemy tried to convince me to give up, telling me that I was sick of this life and that I needed to experience more on the other side of right. I allowed the enemy to plague my mind with feigned injustices and then planned departures because I had the ability and resources to do so. Yet God kept me in my home. God was there when I was a victim of a home invasion by two intruders, (Bishop was asleep), and rather than being subject to violence, rape, or even death, God allowed them to be fearful and almost break their necks running away from me in the dark.

God has kept me!!!! He was there all the time, waiting for me to completely line up. Waiting for me to walk in my call and in His chosen destiny for my life! Oh, how I love Him, oh how I thank Him for never giving up on me! When I look back over my life, I am humbled and stand in complete and utter amazement. For every step, I did and did not take, for every response I did and did not have in life, for everything I am and am not, God was there. He was there not as a non-participating bystander but as one in the game calling the plays and making adjustments as we went along.

I am reminded of the woman that was brought before Jesus accused and guilty of adultery. Without an immediate response, Jesus stooped and began to write in the dirt on the ground. What he wrote, scripture does not tell us. For me, I am convinced that in that writing in the dirt, many years ago, Jesus wrote something for that woman but He also wrote some things into and out of my life. God in His infinite wisdom knew that He would one day use me to be a support to a great leader in His kingdom. As such, there were some things that God erased from my life and others that He inserted. Not based on any goodness in me, but He was keeping me and ensuring that I would not disqualify myself before He got to use me in His master plan. For everything that my regular life has and has not been, God has kept me for such a time as this.

REFLECTION POINTS

"For if you remain silent at this time, relief and deliverance for the Jews will arise from another place, but you and your father's family will perish. And who knows but that you have come to your royal position for such a time as this?"

Esther 4:14 NIV

1. Appointment: All of your life experiences somehow play into your purpose and destiny. What could God possibly be up to right now? Regardless of your present age, what future role might God be shaping you to play in His Kingdom?

2. Divine Connections: How has God currently positioned you to be of assistance to those around you?

_____
_____
_____
_____

3. Assignment: Your time is now. Look around, what is your current assignment?

_____
_____
_____
_____

CHAPTER 2
PILLOW TALK

Pillow talk—people often wonder or worry about pillow talk. What's being said behind closed doors? Pillow talk is the discussion of intimate or private matters in bed or in a relaxed setting, typically with a sexual partner. It's one of the reasons political analysts and the media focus on the 'partners' or spouses of the spotlighted official or celebrity. Pundits are concerned about what's being said to the key person in charge. They seek to understand or be in a position to manipulate those that are closest to the ultimate power. Because of the partner's close proximity and their ability to have a solo audience with the primary person, there is frequently a desire to control what the partner is saying to the primary. It is not often openly discussed, but it is broadly understood that the partner has the ability to persuade or shape the thoughts, actions, and decisions of the primary leader.

What sweet little nothings or great big somethings was Laura whispering to George? What was Hillary saying to Bill and then, what was Bill saying to Hillary? How did Michelle weigh in, in conversations with Barrack, concerning our national economic crisis? What feedback could Melania provide for Donald? Who's influencing whom? Does the influence change with titles or roles? Does the person in front only represent to the public that they are in charge, making all the decisions, or are they the 'shot-caller' in and out of the public's eye? If there is any influence at all, is it a positive persuasion for the promotion and benefit of all people? Or are the subtle suggestions ever so softly sapping the strength of what once was a superpower? These are indeed things that can make you go, "Hmmmm".

In a primary position of authority or importance, the primary or top decision-maker is painfully aware of the impact and the ripple effect that their decisions will have on the lives of those they serve. They are also aware of the persuasive power and influence that those around them can have in shaping their decisions; so they must cautiously choose their advisors. These official advisors must have a clear grasp of the 'Primary's' vision and the goals they are trying to accomplish. Typically, advisors will ensure they keep a Primary current on all matters of importance and will also attempt to shield them against false data and un-vetted speculation, to prevent misinformation that will cloud the primary's thoughts and ultimate actions. However, when the primary is lying down to rest at the end of a long day, that guard is no longer up. In a healthy relationship, there is no longer the perceived power-over scenario, and the primary is no longer guarded but wide open to varied thoughts and propositions. Retiring into private chambers at the end of a long day, battles have been fought, landmines have been cautiously avoided and new routes charted. And, now the primary is home in their family surroundings, the perfect place to be caught off guard and be sabotaged by the enemy.

The primary, in my case, is my husband, the Bishop. Your primary could also be a bishop, pastor, banker, or another key leader in the community. These men of God, like the Bishop, no doubt, have a strong resolve and determination to be informed by their advisors and to do only what God tells them to do. As my husband's partner and wife, I have developed a strong resolve and determination to align with God's will for our lives. However, influence and manipulation can happen easier than you think and you have to constantly guard against being used as the trojan horse that the enemy rides in on. Because of your closeness and the proximity, you have to his heart, your husband will listen to (take in) your thoughts and opinions. Herein lies the danger because if the wife/partner is in any way defiled or bitter, their speech will be tainted and their whisperings under cover will be full of poison to the hearer. Even if the primary verbally rejects what they have heard the damage is done because the very thought has already entered their consciousness and begun to attack their existing thought process. A seed has been planted - good or bad.

Being a cheerleader and supporter is easy when you understand the scope and project; you see the vision; you agree with the direction. You encourage your spouse when others may not or you fill gaps in the ministry to ensure not one part of the plan falls to the ground. Sometimes, however, I do not like the things that God requires Bishop to do. His choice is not my choice or the direction the Bishop has decided is not the way I feel 'led' to go. This is when I must really proceed with caution. It may be within my capability to influence the Bishop, but I must exercise extreme self-control to ensure that I am not swaying him to move in any direction outside of the leading of God's Spirit. Again, yes, he has a strong resolve and determination to do only what God tells him to do. However, we both have to be constantly on guard against the traps of the enemy even when the enemy is in—a-me.

In sleeping with the Bishop, I have to be very careful in what I say and in how and when I chose to say it. My intention would never be to dissuade him from leading exactly how God has called him to lead, on purpose. But the enemy is subtle and full of tricks and schemes. The devil has never told me to fight against my husband to cause division. He has never impressed upon me to refuse support to cause chaos in the ministry. No, I would have immediately rebuked these thoughts and exposed the enemy for what and who he is - a liar, that comes to steal, kill, and destroy. Instead, the devil cautiously and patiently will lay forth his plan to weave a web of deceit and lies that will slowly color my thought process and shape my opinion. Of course, this will be based on what I saw, heard, or felt - firsthand. It couldn't possibly be wrong, right? It would be in his best interest to share all I know, right?

I have come to know that even what we see with our own eyes and hear with our ears can be and often time is a lie from the enemy. The devil wants to influence your thought process so you can be a conduit of defilement for the man of God. It is a pretty clever setup because guards are down and sometimes you don't even recognize you are being used by the devil. This is why we must run everything by God. Lord, this is what I've seen, felt, and heard, how should I process it? What is the truth concerning it? Then you pray and ask God to give you wisdom on how to share what you've uncovered. A spouse loves their mate, and they never want to see them negatively impacted. Particularly in the case of a male, their innate role is to protect and provide coverage. If you come running to your spouse in 'Damsel in Distress' mode, their first response will be to guard and protect, or even to retaliate. This basically just causes distraction from the true issue at hand. Satan is masterful at having us focus on one area while he does his dirt in a different one.

A few years back I had an opportunity to counsel with a pastor concerning the havoc caused in his ministry that ultimately could be traced back to his wife. "Pastor Todd" deeply loved his wife, "Wendy", and felt a deep sense of betrayal just in his approaching me with the issue and the root cause that he was determined to keep from surfacing. Theirs was a fairly new ministry that struggled with membership growth and stability. As visitors came, and some even joined the church, overall, they shared their excitement of being in a place that felt like home. Newcomers expressed that they loved the pastor's warm and genuine personality. Pastor Todd was down-to-earth, plainly spoken, accessible to the congregants, and had an innate ability to make people feel seen and valued. The music ministry was great, and the gospel was easy to understand and apply to everyday life. There was even a fledgling but promising youth program for families with young children.

The pastor shared his hopes and dreams for the mission God had called him to. He proceeded to describe the beautiful people that came in and how many of them got to work serving, almost right away. Though he beamed with pride as he described the people coming in and the work of the ministry, I could tell he was avoiding and even delaying telling me about his assessment of what was causing people to leave. I gently prodded, in an attempt to move the conversation along, "Pastor, it seems the people love God, the programs your ministry has to offer, they certainly love you, what is your assessment of the problem?" The pace of his words quickened and became strained, it looked as if he would be sick sitting right there at my desk. Instead, he went into defense mode.

My wife is a beautifully saved woman of God that has overcome a lot! She has the voice of an angel and can really teach the word of God, sometimes I think even better than I do. She is my number one supporter and is at every event the church puts on. She does all this without complaint and works a full-time job. I don't know where she gets all of the energy, and I am not quite sure what I would do without her. This entire thing was said almost without taking a breath and it ended as abruptly as it started. He stared at me to see if I would dare question what he had said or maybe even if I believed all that he said. There were a few ways I could go with this. I sat in silence processing more so what he did not say and what was missing from the previous testimony of the members.

Choosing not to deal with the statement that he wasn't sure what to do without his wife, I asked Pastor Todd about the relationship his wife had with the congregants. Though it indeed seemed as if she loved and supported him, I could not tell where she was in her interactions with the people. Eventually, I learned that though Wendy was supportive of the programs and congregants in their presence she often had critical things to say to her husband about their performance or their intent, in the privacy of their home. Wendy had grown up in a home that was chock full of secrecy and deceit and unfortunately, it seemed, much of her upbringing marred and informed her interactions with others. As we minister to others, including our husbands, we must allow God to mend our broken places, so we are pouring out wholeness and soundness of mind.

Careless and unchecked words dropped here and there had caused Pastor Todd to question his leadership team or suspect them of ulterior motives. The confidence that Pastor Todd once had in his small staff began to deteriorate. He began seeing the people through his wife's eyes rather than the way he initially saw them, through God's eyes. Through the grace and mercy of God, it was revealed that the pastor was becoming more and more critical in nature versus his initial style of encouragement. Just like that, the enemy had quietly crept in, using the voice of his beautiful wife, and was negatively impacting the way the pastor was leading and ultimately the morale of the congregation.

I occasionally see Pastor Todd, but he has not brought up this matter, so neither have I. I would have loved to minister to Wendy and encourage her to do good work, however, I never got to speak directly to her. I often think of Wendy and the countless other Wendys like her. My prayer for her and those that find themselves in the same position is that they first and foremost allow God to heal them from all past offenses and brokenness, no matter the source. I pray that we recognize the power we have in our positions and the responsibility to carefully guard what we speak to our husbands. I hear the scripture that reminds us that all things lawful are not expedient. We simply do not have to give breath to every thought that enters our minds. I pray that we recognize the enemy a thousand miles away and refuse to be used as a pawn to destroy any portion of God's work.

Pillow talk. Watch your mouth. Choose your words carefully. Although you are not in the White House, you have the ability to shape nations. What you speak to your mate will color their perception, thoughts, and opinions. "God, what am I saying or not saying that will adversely impact the direction of this ministry?" "What am I talking about while lying on our pillows at night?" Seeking God first keeps everything in proper perspective and the words that come out of your mouth can be instruments to build up instead of weapons to tear down.

REFLECTION POINTS

"May these words of my mouth and this meditation of my heart be pleasing in your sight, Lord, my Rock and my Redeemer."

Psalm 19:14 NIV

"A person's words can be a source of wisdom, deep as the ocean, fresh as a flowing stream."

Proverbs 18:4 GNT

1. Influence: How do you respond when someone shares their hopes and dreams? How are you controlling the thoughts of your heart?

2. Your opinion matters: What precautions have you put in place to ensure your spoken words are not selfish or tainted but are filled with wisdom flowing as a fresh stream?

CHAPTER 3

JEHOVAH WAKE-HIM-UP

When Abraham, in the Old Testament, was called to sacrifice his son, seemingly at the last minute, God provided a ram caught in a bush. Abraham named the place Jehovah-Jireh because God revealed himself to Abraham as a provider (Genesis 22:14). As the Children of Israel wandered through the wilderness, on their way to the Promised Land, they were also exposed to the nature and character of God. At Rephidim, Moses ordered Joshua to battle when the Amalekites came against them. God was revealed as Jehovah Nissi - he was their banner of victory over the Amalekites.

Though God continues to reveal himself to us in many ways, we have stopped naming him as such because we now know his name and we call him Jesus. Every now and then, however, when God does something particularly astounding, I like to mirror the patriarchs of the Old Testament and name God, according to something he has revealed to me. Just the other day, I came to know him as Jehovah Wakehimup. That's pronounced 'Wake-Him-Up.' Oh yes, and I do give him glory!

My husband and I work in ministry together and we often move so fast that by the end of the day we are simply exhausted. Many days, thoughts of intimacy run through our minds but by the end of the day, we just have no more energy to see the thought through to reality. I cannot speak for his side but as for what's going on with me, ladies are you out there? Shout amen if you know where I'm going! You know how it is. You see him throughout the day and for the most part, you are trying all you know how to serve God in the gifts he has given you. You also admire the God in him (your husband). You see your spouse in action, you pray for him, you pray with him; you support him, complete tasks for him, attend sessions together, share meals on the go, witness God work through him delivering the word, serving the people, spending time with youth, working in the community, breaking through barriers, etc. You see what God is doing through the ministry and your spouse and you think, "God you are truly amazing". At some point, however, every now and again, your mind and emotions (feelings) shift. In addition to thinking how great God is, you begin to have a different sort of 'stirring' and begin to think Ummm, I love that man - all of him.

Now, this may mess some of you up, but instead of just that "I love you with the love of the Lord" feeling all of Sister Eros will come flooding in. You begin to think, "When is our next break in the day?" Or "What time will we get home tonight?" Now all of a sudden you pray with new intensity, "God move whatever needs to be moved to hurry this meeting along because I have another ministry that is waiting for me at home!" You have to focus harder on what God is presently trying to accomplish because now that, 'that' thought has formed in your mind, every move he makes, every casual touch, can be a distraction to what you should be focused on.

What exciting days those are in ministry! The challenge comes in that often the days just don't get any shorter. By the time we roll into our home sanctuary I am exhausted, he is exhausted. Many nights we get ready for bed and fall in, almost sleeping before our heads hit the pillow. If either of us has one more letter to write or proof, one more email to check, a load of clothes that should be started, by the time the other gets into the room they are greeted with the cursed sound of snoring!

As life would have it, however, we are not always on the exact same page. Sometimes I get a quick nap in, in the middle of the day. Sometimes he has fallen asleep while waiting for a meeting to begin and has a small amount of reserve left in the evening. You feel the 'signal' (maybe a foot or a hand coming over towards the other person), in your mind you are pleased, and you think you are responding only to awake the next morning wondering what happened the night before - once again, you fell asleep.

When I'm on the side of being awake and he's asleep I hate it. I've got a few tricks up my sleeve and over the years a lot of things have worked. However, the older the Bishop gets, it seems to be harder and harder to wake him up, once asleep. This brings me to our great and awesome God. Lying in bed one night, I determined that I did not want to go to sleep, and I absolutely wanted him to wake up. Almost as a fluke, I said, in my mind, "God wake him up!" Now for the sake of my readers, I will spare you the details, but I told God what I wanted and 'how' I wanted the Bishop to wake up. It seemed to me that out of a deep and heavy sleep the Bishop woke up, in all his splendor. Oh my God, I now know you to be Jehovah Wake Him Up!!! Because who but God could whisper into his son's ear, wake him out of sound slumber, and have him meet all of my specified needs?!

We say that there is nothing too hard for God and that he cares about every aspect of our lives. Yet, it took me 32 years of marriage to pray this simple prayer, "God, wake him up". What is it you need in your marriage? Do you need him to be Jehovah Bringhimhome? Or, do you need God to be Jehovah Restorethelove? God has done many things for me in and through my marriage. We know to go to him for the 'big' things in our lives. I just want to remind you that God cares about every facet of your marriage. If you are struggling in any area, tell God about it and see how he wants to reveal himself to you.

REFLECTION POINTS

"But my God shall supply all your need according to His riches in glory by Christ Jesus."

Philippians 4:19 KJV

1. Name it and claim it: What impossible or improbable situations have you failed to acknowledge God by naming the outcome?

2. Discover God in new ways: Name Him Jehovah (fill in the blank).

3. Do you tend to ask God only for things you can visualize? What crazy thing can you seek God for?

CHAPTER 4

ENEMIES CAMP

Does anybody, other than me, sit through some church services scolding yourself? I mean tonight I am sitting here, of course on the front row, a guest invited to a friend's program, smiling, and looking thrilled to be here, deep in the service, and I absolutely would prefer not to be here. Sometimes, I think I am one of the few First Ladies (pastor's wives) that do not love to spend their every waking moment in somebody's church service. Whew! I am working really hard to say, sometimes I just don't want to go to one more church service, especially on Sunday. We are running two services - 9 am and 11 am, per Sunday, and to go to a third (and sometimes fourth) service at 3:00 pm or 7:00 pm, is just not what I want to do. The struggle comes in because God is always worthy of praise and for sure, as a First Lady I should always be willing to worship God on any occasion, at any time, and all the time. Right? Help me, Lord. I promise I love God, but sometimes, I do not want to go to one more Anniversary, Appreciation, Women's Day, Usher's Day, Choir Day, Revival, or any of the other 'special' services, that we can come up with. I mean, after all, did not these people worship God during their regular service times? But, I digress.

So tonight, I am sitting in service, and, having silenced the running narrative in my head, I am actually enjoying service, making the best of being here. After all, this service is hosted by one of my good friends. We often go to lunch with a few other pastors' wives and share ministry ideas and a few good laughs. We've made it through prayer, praise, and worship, and a few words of exhortation for the audience to get up, clap, shout, give God praise, high-five someone, and dance our best dance for 60 seconds. By the way, does anyone other than me feel that sometimes people may be just saying and doing these things because you commanded them to, and not really because they are reverencing or praising God? Do most people, when commanded to shout and tell God, "Yes!", stop and elevate their thoughts towards God, and commit to saying Yes, to Him? Or, are we just parroting what we heard, with no real thought of actually talking to God? Wow, I am straying again. Perhaps you get the picture of how I had to continually fight to stay focused on Jesus in this service.

At some point, I really began to give God praise. A praise dance came forward, "The Battle Is Not Yours, It's The Lord's". The presence of God came in and began ministering to me personally. I could feel God's Spirit. The lyrics of the song came to a place where the dancer illustrated the words of the song in how God can take you around the enemy's camp and hide you ... That's when I clearly heard it. God spoke softly and said to me, "This is what I have done for you". What? Now, these are the only words I heard, but I intuitively knew that God was speaking concerning my sitting in this very service, having been invited by my 'friend'. God was saying my 'friend' was actually my enemy, and yet He 'hides' or protects me as he takes me around their presence (camp).

I was immobilized; frozen dead at the moment. It seemed as if everything in the room stopped moving and the air had been knocked out of me. What were the connotations? I immediately wanted to be hurt and leave. I felt used. Only a few months earlier, I was happy to meet this co-laborer in the gospel, for lunch. To my surprise, there were a couple of other individuals there when I arrived. We all exchanged pleasantries and I inwardly wondered what the real agenda was. In retrospect, there were faint warnings of caution that I did not quite understand. The conversation, after I was seated, seemed to pick up from a place that I was not privy to so initially, I just sat and smiled. After all, I was the newcomer, the others had served together in the area for some time. There were nudges for me to join in and give my perspective on events that I had no knowledge of and frankly, was not comfortable speaking on. I remained present in the conversation with body language but had very little to add other than an occasional "hmm" or "oh my". Eventually, a couple of the other ladies picked up on my non-participatory or non-additive remarks and the topic turned solely to my church, Victory In Praise (VIP). They wanted to know how we were structured, what we were planning next, and what we taught our leadership team. The questions went on for a while and I, thinking there was genuine interest in ministry building, gave my best and most detailed responses. I believe that we should all serve to the best of our ability in the kingdom and I totally believe the iron sharpens iron concept. Sitting there at the table, so I would not later forget, I shared with them our meeting agendas, strategy plans, and work plans for our leadership team, through email. After some time, I noticed I was doing all of the talking and the ladies were primarily just listening. They would occasionally respond by saying, "Oh, we've done that before," or "That's not going to work here." The lunch meeting came to an end and as I got up, I realized none of them shared anything they were working on in their ministry. I innocently wondered if I had monopolized all the time.

Hearing clearly, that I was in the enemy's camp, I thought back to all of the ministry tips and processes, that I so openly shared. I vividly remembered answering their questions, like it was a movie reel playing before my eyes. Though I now understood that their silence, while I shared, was total disdain or indifference for my material. At the lunch table, there had only been smiles and flattering words, shared with me directly. Sitting here now, in this building, this is the enemies camp? I struggled with how I should feel and more importantly, what would I say to this person, now that God had revealed their true self to me.

I felt God impressing on me that I would say or do nothing. He had already fought my battle and would continue to fight them. I was instructed to continue to love, continue to share, and continue to support their ministry. This was not my battle to fight. I could not help but wonder why I needed to know the truth, concerning this fellow woman of God. God responded by reminding me that it is easy to love, lovely people. Now, he wanted me to grow up and love, not so lovely people - the prickly ones. God wanted me to see my friend, no quotes around the word, for all she was, and wasn't, and to make the fully-aware choice, of loving her, nevertheless. This could not be a diminished love, in any way. Love is not dependent upon whether or not love is returned. Contrary to popular sentiment, love is not, technically, a two-way street. Love is one-directional. God loves us unconditionally, and I knew I had to love unconditionally, as well.

How simple and naive I must have seemed to my friend, that night. For with clear revelation from God, I stood, I worshipped; hands lifted high, with occasional tears of joy. At that moment, I was overcome with the weight of God's love for me. The more love, gratitude, and attention that I gave to my Savior, the more He lavished His love on me. Others couldn't have known it but my Protector, my Shepherd, had set a table and prepared a sumptuous meal before me, right in the very presence of my enemy, and I went all in, enjoying every moment.

REFLECTION POINTS

"You prepare a feast for me in the presence of my enemies. You honor me by anointing my head with oil. My cup overflows with blessings."

Psalms 23:5 NLT

1. Challenge: How difficult is it for you to serve prickly people or those who have misused you?

2. Love your enemies: What blessings might you be missing out on by only loving those that you deem worthy of love?

CHAPTER 5

THINGS THAT GO BUMP IN THE NIGHT

"Authorities on Friday identified four men arrested after a daylong search prompted by two home invasion robberies in Northern California that left a man dead and another wounded."

"A violent group of burglars disrupted a family's quiet evening at home. Although seven family members were home at the time of the robbery, it did not deter the armed group of robbers. The suspects pistol whipped and physically drugged some victims. Threatening to kill them, the robbers demanded the family to give them their valuables."

Just a quick and easy web search of 'Home Invasions' will produce many, many articles of reported burglaries, such as the two quoted samples above. Names and cities were removed to protect the victims.

The US Department of Justice in a Special Report, according to the most recent statistics from the Department of Justice, shows that 3.7 million homes are broken into each year. One million of those burglaries are home invasions.

In California, when a person commits the crime of burglary by entering a building in order to commit a crime inside, is sometimes called a home invasion burglary. In other words, someone has had the audacity to come into your private domain, uninvited, unwelcomed, and in most cases, unknown.

I often think of Psalm 127:1 (with added emphasis on the second part), *"Unless it is the Lord who builds the house, the builders' work is pointless. Unless it is the Lord who protects the city, the guard on duty is pointless."*

I believe we should make a practice of locking windows and doors and ensuring we are taking all the necessary precautions to protect our families and homes. However, our total trust and dependence cannot rest solely on the alarm system we may have installed. Alarms fail. Windows can be 'jimmied' open. Door locks can be picked. Many of the burglaries that occur, happen regardless of locked doors and windows, alarms, or other safety measures. Despite your best efforts to protect your family, it is God alone who has the power to provide total protection - unless it is the Lord who protects the 'city', the guard on duty is pointless.

My daughter had just gotten married on Saturday. It was a beautiful wedding, and our family and friends were very generous in blessing her and her husband. The reception went late, and the decision was made to transport all the unopened gifts to my house until the newlyweds returned from their honeymoon vacation.

At the end of the day, Bishop and I expressed our love and thanks and bid farewell to our friends and out-of-town guests. Arriving back at our home, we unpacked and carefully stacked the mounds of presents in our family room around the fireplace. Looking at the enormity of it all we once again wondered if our children could truly know that they were recipients of the favor of God that flowed down to them, from our lives. We straightened up a bit from all of the harried activity until we had no more strength to do one more thing. My husband and I crashed into our beds without too much conversation, utterly exhausted from all the joyous celebration.

As soon as my head hit the pillow, I fell into a deep and welcomed sleep. At some point, some misplaced, yet familiar sound caused me to stir, threatening to pull me out of my much-needed rest. My first waking thought was, "Why are *they* in the china cabinet?" After the thought, I begin to realize the ridiculousness of it. "Why in the world *would* they be?. . wait, what *they*?" The noise I heard was distinct, I knew it well. It was the sound of my china cabinet being opened. (I am a collector of Princess House and a few other crystal pieces.) "What time is it? Why do they need crystal?"

Still very much in a fog, not having moved from my comfortable sleeping position, the next sound I heard was the linen closet right outside my door open with the familiar scraping sound of wood against wood - caused by the children swinging on the door over the years. New thoughts, "They need a blanket???? Who? Why?" All of this time the thought in the back of my mind is that one of the 'kids' (both had keys) had come home, and I could not, for the life of me, figure out what this abnormal pattern of behavior meant.

Well, I'm going to have to get up to see what was going on. I remember hoping it wasn't Tia - having missed her flight. (Another nonsensical thought because they had their own apartment, if so.) I threw on a robe and walked out of the door of my room. The first thing I heard was a male voice exclaiming, "Oh, shoot!" Only he didn't say shoot it was that other expletive that 100% woke me up. There was no longer any confusion. Though my children (still waiting, at the time of this writing, for them to be saved) may or may not have used profanity outside my house, neither of them used it inside my house. I was now wide awake. Three feet in front of me, standing at my linen closet, dressed in dark clothing, was a man I had never seen in my life. Movement caught my eye below and there was a second man, dressed similarly, standing in my formal dining room below.

You have got to be kidding me! I was immediately angered. I begin to scream for Rufus and charge toward the individual. "What are you doing in my house!" I demanded. "Rufus, there is someone in my house!" Yes, I, for whatever reason said, my house! Because I was now so close to the individual, he pushed past me and ran down the stairs, with me in hot pursuit. No glasses, no contacts, pitch black house, and here I go, screaming after him, "What are you doing? Rufus!"

By the time my dear husband - the Bishop, got his clothes on (what????) and came out of the room, I had chased both intruders out the window they had come in. They jumped over our back fence, which backed up to a levy and was long gone. In total shock and disbelief at what just occurred, we called the police.

The police arrived and checked outside and around the perimeter of the house. They were gone. They found a vase outside and a small crystal figurine. The men left muddy footprints on my white carpet but no fingerprints. I could tell that the two figurines were all they had moved from the china cabinet because there was a slight dust ring as evidence of the place the pieces once stood. The intruders simply slid open a sliding window and let themselves in. Our alarm system failed to alert us because apparently, the contact had become worn, over the years, and no longer served its intended purpose. We now remind everyone that if you are not checking your system once every 30 days you may invalidate any claim.

Here's how good God is at protecting our possessions. Not two feet from the china cabinet, right through the arches and into our family room next door, was an undisturbed mound of wrapped treasures. I could almost not believe it - almost. God, you hid the treasures from their sight. They spent all that time looking at old Princess House dishes and collectibles, that only mattered to me, and failed to spot all the gifts from my daughter's wedding! The burglars apparently went on a search for blankets in a closet upstairs, and even going up and down the stairs did not shine a light on the treasure trove that they had access to. In addition to the wedding gifts, just around the corner were our computers, autographed hanging artwork, a new flat screen television, and other things of great value, all almost within arms reach. Based on the carpet stains from their muddy footprints, they never even headed in that direction. God, did you place a warring angel there at the threshold? Did you blind their eyes and just have them see utter darkness, instead of the wrapping and sparkly bows?

The responding officers were just as astonished as we were that the 'night raiders' missed out on their opportunity for more. Once that conversation subsided the officers had me repeat what occurred and I had to show them where the men stood and retrace my steps. Shocked at my response they began to chastise me concerning my actions of chasing the burglars from my home. They wanted to know what was I thinking. I wasn't. Once again, the realization and enormity of God's grace and protection became very clear. I had no weapon, no special training, and I certainly had no plan. In the years that followed, each time I would hear of a report of injury or loss of life during a home invasion, I would be reminded of how God covered me in my actions. He is a powerful God and well-able, despite poor choices, to keep us safe from the things that go bump in the night.

REFLECTION POINTS

"Unless the LORD protects a city, guarding it with sentries will do no good."

Psalm 127:1b NLT

1. God is our present help in times of trouble: How has God helped you and provided safety in times of calamity?

2. Looking back over your life, where might there have been times that God supernaturally blocked something that could have or should have happened?

CHAPTER 6
MISS MINISTRY

Yesterday was one of the sickest days of my life. At least it seemed that way to me. I had been struggling with hay fever, and various types of colds and now it seemed I had a sinus infection. My face was swollen on one side and hurt to lie on or touch. My nose was stopped up and it was extremely painful to attempt to blow it. I was running a temperature and feeling quite nauseous, more than likely from the whole barrage of medication I was taking, in an attempt to feel better. My mouth stayed dry, I was cold and then hot. My muscles ached and I felt extremely weak at one point I felt all strength seem to drain out of me.

My grandson, age six at the time, did all he could to bring me water, blankets, and tissue, and try to get me to let him make some tea and a sandwich. Later in the day, when my mom found out I was ill, she brought me hot compresses and then a hot water bottle for my face. Mom went to Kaiser and picked up a prescription for antibiotics for me. My sisters, Cheryl and Wilma (childhood friend, turned sister for life) called a couple of times to see what they could bring me - food, juice, medicine? My oldest sister brought me Halls's throat lozenges, which was the only other thing I could think of that may give some relief.

Where was the Bishop? Somewhere with Miss Ministry—no doubt. Who is Miss Ministry? Why she is all of the never-ending demands of ministry that I have personified as the other woman. Miss Ministry has several of the same attributes as a mistress; taking up all of his time, and demanding all of his attention. She can bring him joy and cause him pain and sorrow. Miss Ministry is on Bishop's mind all of the time. It is not uncommon for me to see things that were purchased for me, now in the hands of Miss Ministry - a flat-screen television, my beautiful large house plant, my ornate mirror, the shop vac. Many things have been taken from our home, and given to Miss Ministry because she needs them. Bishop pampers and coddles her, consistently spends large amounts of money on her, and occasionally forgets he had a 'honey-do list, for me, his wife, all because of this mistress.

What is really going on? I am not a sickly person. I seldom stop my schedule for the luxury of actually curling up somewhere to die, when I am feeling under the weather. Matter of fact, earlier that day I kept a commitment I made to visit my niece's school to sit in on a couple of classes where she was having some difficulty. I even ended up playing volleyball with one of the classes. However, I left the school and soon thereafter knew that being out in the air even for that brief period was not the right thing for me. I felt worse than ever.

Now, just perhaps the Bishop thought I was all better since I went to my niece's school before he left home that morning. I want to give him that. However, he did know I had been struggling with some sort of virus for about a week. Today, much like any other day, he left home in the morning, rushing off to meet the demands of Miss Ministry, and never called back to check on me. He eventually came home after 10 p.m.

Here is the challenge and yes, the struggle. I absolutely wanted to have an attitude and be angry with him for what I felt was a lack of care and concern. Once again, I was playing second fiddle to 'Miss Ministry.' It seems more and more she gets top billing no matter what crisis I seem to have in life! Yes, I had everything I needed. Yes, I have the gift of healing. Yes, I had others available and calling me, that know how to get a prayer through. And, yes, eventually the worst of it subsided around 9 p.m. and I was able to rest and have some relief. None of that is the point!

I did not care who needed what, who was having a breakdown, what marriage was falling apart, which individual needed counseling, what meeting needed facilitating, or what team had to be led! Because after all, that is what ministry is all about and it never ends! Today should have been about me!

Okay, in truth I would not have let him miss one session or meeting. All I really wanted, *needed* was a phone call to ask how I was doing and to see if I needed anything. The thing I needed from him was attention and recognition that you are not doing so well today! I love the ministry. I am not insecure and do not battle or pull the Bishop, causing inner turmoil for him. And most days we are both so busy we check in with each other as we can, especially if we are not somewhere serving together.

I think what was ironic was that when the Bishop came home that evening, after a challenge of ministering to a husband in the ministry, where the wife had decided that she wanted a divorce and was unwilling to come in for counseling. She was fed up! With what, they wondered? Bishop had spent time that very day counseling a couple whose marriage was headed for trouble because of their roles in youth ministry. Hmmm, I said to myself. I was not confused as to why there are always so many issues within marriage, in the body of Christ. Miss Ministry is demanding and oftentimes she screams for first place in the lives of those that serve her.

In ministry, you must always, always make sure that your marriage is strong and fortified against the attacks of Miss Ministry. I know for sure that I was acting like a brat. As ugly as I made everything sound, I know without a doubt that one call to the Bishop would have brought him directly to my aid. He esteems me highly; I am his queen and do not doubt my placement in our castle. Our relationship is strong; we are each other's support and confidante. So, the scary part is that if the enemy (that is exactly who was at work) could make me want to throw a tantrum and have an attitude when I am not confused about my role in marriage and ministry, what about those that are just getting started? What about those that already struggle with insecurities?

Husbands, and wives, pour into your spouses all you know how. When you have light days in ministry, make sure you are making deposits into your spouse's emotional bank account. Take the time to meet for breakfast or lunch. Send a card—for no special reason. Bring home flowers or make a special treat. Arrange a mini-vacation and kidnap your spouse. Take a class together that will force time spent together. This can be a salsa class or a finance class, it does not matter. Record your favorite show and do not watch it until you commit to a time you will sit down together each week to watch. Practice laughing and smiling more, have fun, and don't always be so serious. Miss Ministry will never just stop and give you time to do something, you have to be assertive and take the time to minister to each other's needs.

Taking the time to invest in your spouse will ensure that when ministry is running at a hectic pace, and you happen to miss some key opportunities to spoil your mate, it will not be so detrimental. Because of all the previous deposits, you will not break the bank and emotionally bankrupt the relationship. I pray for a healthy balance in every marriage that is involved with ministry. This is not an expectation of equal parts but the 'right' amounts of time, based on what the individuals need and based on ministry requirements according to the maturity level of the ministry.

REFLECTION POINTS

"An unmarried man can spend his time doing the Lord's work and thinking how to please him. But a married man can't do that so well. He has to think about his earthly responsibilities and how to please his wife. His interests are divided. In the same way, a woman who is no longer married or has never been married can be more devoted to the Lord in body and spirit, while the married woman must be concerned about her earthly responsibilities and how to please her husband."
1 Corinthians 7:32-34 NLT

1. What practices have you put in place to ensure Miss Ministry does not consume all of your time and rob you of enjoyment in your marriage?

2. Discuss with your spouse, in advance, the best method to signify times you are feeling under-appreciated, because of the business of ministry. Create a plan together to rectify this.

CHAPTER 7
IT ADDS NO SORROW

"Oh, you shouldn't have! No, I really mean it - you really should not have. It's free, you say. Yes, but how much will it really cost?" In Proverbs 16:2, the psalmist writes, "The blessings of God are rich and add no sorrow." That, then, must be the gauge whereby we can tell if the 'thing' we were just given is indeed a blessing.

Here I sit, once again, having returned from a 'free' weekend getaway, only to have to watch Bishop balance our checking account and rearrange household finances to cover all of the 'free' things that were not so free. Hmmm. The hotel, this time was free, as was the transportation. But let's see, we have the cost of meals, the cost of entertainment, porter fees, shuttle fees, and the like, that any way you slice it, was just not part of our budget before we were 'blessed' with this much-needed rest.

A while back we were 'blessed' with round-trip airline tickets to New York! Wahoo, this is a favorite vacation spot for us. We should have asked more questions but somehow, we assumed it would include hotel and meal allowance because the flight arrangements had us in NY for eight days. I am not sure if you've stayed in NY in a while but our average accommodation room was over $400 per night. We weren't called to a fast, so we needed to eat every day, at least once. Yes, our weakness is Broadway - which is why the destination was chosen for us, I'm sure because everyone knows we love the theatre. So, after a few $125 tickets, per person to Broadway, the cab fees, metro fees, and minimal shopping - we were set back for easily $4K. I guess to make matters worse (we had the time of our lives though!), we had just gotten home from a family vacation with our adult children and grandson. In other words, this free trip could not have come at a worse time. We were already having to recover financially. This free trip put us in a financial hole.

I kept saying, "For sure, we will be reimbursed after we get back - don't worry about it." This may have been why we went ahead and picked up an item or two while shopping. Well, the weeks went by, and no one asked or inquired, in the least, about the expenses. Hmmm, I feel some sorrow. Then, just perhaps, this wasn't a blessing.

What would it look like to you, if you offered or saw someone offer 'free' tickets to a concert or a different type of event, or even to a vacation destination and the person declined? Would you think the recipient is ungrateful? Would you think it a shame and that the person was being rude? There are just not a lot of graceful ways to ask questions concerning a free gift. However, when questions are not asked there can be many surprise price tags attached.

I recall in the Word of God where a question is asked, "Which of you goes to war without first counting the cost? I am learning to be appreciative of the intent of a gift but also to ask more questions. Even if a gift is not well thought out you still do not want the well-intentioned gift-giver to waste their resources that you may never use. Be grateful and appreciative but if it is not clearly spelled out ask questions, "Wow, this sounds great! Thank you so much for thinking of us. Is the airfare included? Will we have transportation when we arrive? Has the hotel been arranged?" All of this may seem like you are pushing to receive more. However, what you are doing, upfront is establishing, though you are grateful for the gift, it will have to be placed on hold until provisions will be made to cover all expenses. If not, people may wonder why you have not utilized their gift and think you didn't like their gift or worse that you don't like them. There is a widespread belief that the pastors/bishops all have money to fill in the gap for whatever was not received. Of course, if money is not an issue for you, no worries, accept the gift and make up the difference.

This is not the case for a great number of pastors/bishops. We have budgets that have already been planned, we are already stretched by assisting other households, and we have adult children that are oftentimes still in our pockets. So yes, we appreciate the gift, but a gift really should not come with any hidden price tags. When my husband gives me a gift, I do not expect to come out of pocket for any part of it, or it was not a gift. Anything that is truly a gift should not have a monthly charge associated, that I now have to adjust my budget and pay!

I've heard another common 'gift' in the body of Christ is where a church representative will hold a program or banquet for their pastor or an honoree and take all the meal costs and program expenses out of the proceeds for the honoree. So, they have multiple paid guests, then they comp multiple meals (free), hire consultants and assistants, and with what is left they advise the pastor/honoree that the committee will hold the balance for them. If they need anything, they should just ask. So, is this like an allowance? Is your pastor still in grade school? So, you are going to hold on to what you've said was the pastor's / honoree's money and then require that they come to you to ask for it when they feel they need it? Yeah, no thanks. This is not a gift, and no one wants their money held or to be controlled in this manner.

So, the next time you want to give a gift to your man or woman of God, first of all, make sure you are being led by God to do so. Your gifts should not be for public shows. They should not be to gain favor or anything else of that nature. God promises that he would bless those that bless Him and show favor unto His people. If God is calling you to be the one, he chooses to bless His servant, then do it as God has ordained, to the best of your ability.

Consider not only what you spend and give but also consider what it will cost the recipients to use your gift. If you give a car, consider whether or not the pastor can afford insurance, gas, maintenance, does he have a garage to put it in. You get the picture. Will he be excited about the car and then be stressed each month about the increased insurance that has to be paid? If you provide airline tickets, make sure you have researched the average cost of hotels for the area and either book and pay for the hotel or provide the money for the hotel, including all of the many hotel surcharges. Will they need a rental car? Transportation to and from the airport? Remember the meal allowance for the duration of the stay for breakfast, lunch, and dinner. The best gifts are well thought out and planned, in advance.

There will be times when you simply will not have the resources to take care of everything that is needed. Guess what? They may not be able to either. In this case, it is a better idea to bless your leader with either a gift card or cash. Let them decide how and when to spend it. If you have truly prayed, as recommended, it will be an exact answer to a need or a desire your pastor has. If your pastor, in turn, blesses someone else with it, just know that you were faithful in doing as God instructed you. Money is considered currency because it flows in and out. Don't worry about where or how the current flow once it leaves your hands. When giving gifts to your leader, be determined to do all you can to be that blessing that will add no sorrow.

REFLECTION POINTS

"The blessing of the LORD makes a person rich, and he adds no sorrow with it."

Proverbs 10:22 NLT

"For which of you, intending to build a tower, does not sit down first and count the cost, whether he has enough to finish it—lest, after he has laid the foundation, and is not able to finish, all who see it begin to mock him, saying, 'This man began to build and was not able to finish'? Or what king, going to make war against another king, does not sit down first and consider whether he is able with ten thousand to meet him who comes against him with twenty thousand?"

Luke 14:28-31 NKJV

1. Gift givers: Have you received a gift that later cost you extra finances to maintain it? How did this alter the way you felt about the gift or the gift-giver?

2. Gift receivers: How might 'impulse gifts' be more likely to cause sorrow, in the long run?

CHAPTER 8
NO MORE CHURCH

I am so fed up, sick, and tired of church! I tremble at even putting this in print because I know there is not another single solitary wife, of those in ministry that feels the way I do. Yeah, right! I know you are out there but like me usually choose to remain silent and just smile. Please do know that I truly love the Lord, all I know how. And, I am learning to love Him more every day. But despite my desire to be pleasing unto God, there are just those days, when I have had it! I do not want to see the church, church people, people that act or talk like church people, none of it! There has got to be more in life than getting up and going from meeting to meeting, from session to session, to bible study, to practice, to rehearsal, to prayer, to church, to home (to discuss the meetings, practices, and church) just to wake up and do it all over again! Oh, my Lord, please not again today!!! God, is this really your will? Does it take all of this? Am I a heathen for wanting something more or at least different?

I want to go to the movies. I want to take a long walk on the beach. I want to sleep in late and have breakfast in bed. I then want someone else to come and clean it up. I want to have a day where I drive without knowing where I will end up. I want to have days when I don't see the church building. I want to go rummaging through antique shops. I want to watch the back roads of America on television and then have the time and ability to go and personally visit the places. And more than anything, I want my husband to want those things and to have the time (without guilt) to do them.

I woke up one day and just thought, "Not today. I cannot spend another full day at the church." I rode with the Bishop to the morning bible study and as it was time to get out, I told him I was not going in today. He looked at me like I was saying instead I was going to go and make sacrifices to the sun god or something. I wasn't renouncing Christianity or anything; I just did not want to go to the morning bible study that would be followed by meetings, which would be followed by youth resource time, which would be followed by evening bible study. As he got out of the car though, there was for the briefest of moments a look in his eye that said, "I'm not sure I want to go either."

What do you do when you plain get tired of church? Has this not happened to anyone else? At my secular job, I would take a day or a week off work. And in that case, usually, my director or peers would not call me to see if I would take just one quick meeting. But ministry is not convenient, and it is not on a schedule. I came in one day from working a golf tournament. We were up at 5 a.m. to set up for the event. We greeted and entertained all day. I was applauded for being upbeat and the life of the party. It was a very warm day, and I came home, tired and dirty. Because all of life is a rush, I left some incomplete 'matters' at home that required my immediate attention. I took care of them, one by one, all the while promising myself a good hot shower and bed at an early hour.

Just as I was nearing the end of all of my "have-to-dos," (the shower was close in sight) I received a text telling me that one of the members was in the emergency in excruciating pain. "God, for real?" This would have been an easy call if it was one of those that had a 'regular' crisis. Them, I've learned to pray for, over the phone, believe God hears and answers prayers, and go on with my day. No, this was one that never calls, and probably did not know the text was sent on their behalf. She is faithful and goes above and beyond to serve in the ministry wherever she can. Nevertheless, there was a struggle because my flesh was exhausted, but my spirit said, you have got to go. "God, help me". I took my shower but instead of getting prepared for bed, I re-dressed, and the Bishop and I headed out to the hospital. We were able to get in and see her, pray, and were back home within the hour.

I remember feeling good in my spirit for being able to minister to the individual in her time of need. God, this is truly what you called us to do. Regardless of what flesh feels, we are willing vessels, willing to be used by you. We sing a song that says, "If you can use anything, Lord, you can use me." Usually, we just get caught up in the rhythm and melody and sing the song with meaning, feeling, and gusto. I have learned that oftentimes, God will test us in what we preach and what we sing about. When we sing about God using our hands and our feet, we had better mean it. When we ask God to use us, we better mean it.

God reminded me that what we are doing is not just about 'church.' We are serving in ministry, fulfilling our purpose, changing lives, and expanding the kingdom of God. When we go in our own strength, we can become overburdened and grow weary. When we are just 'doing' church we will become drained and have all of our energy sucked right out of us. Just that quick prayer, "God, help me," gave me the strength I needed to go and minister to the sick.

This was in the early days before there were pastoral staff teams within the ministry that was on rotational call for service. Sometimes now, God still prompts us to be the ones to personally respond and of course, we will. Back then, the church had not grown in size nor in spiritual maturity where others were ready to be sent on assignment. If there was a call, we were the ones to respond. Regardless of the size of our ministry, God wants us to remember to allow His Spirit to fill us, new and fresh, for each new task, for each new day. Smaller churches have pressing issues and challenges and as churches grow larger, I've seen that there are different and usually greater challenges. Either way, when we learn to go in God's power, He will renew our strength to accomplish each and every assignment that He calls us to.

REFLECTION POINTS

"He gives power to the weak and strength to the powerless. Even youths will become weak and tired, and young men will fall in exhaustion. But those who trust in the LORD will find new strength. They will soar high on wings like eagles. They will run and not grow weary. They will walk and not faint."

Isaiah 40:29-31 NLT

1. How, when, and where were you called to serve in ministry? Recall the specifics.

_____

_____

_____

_____

2. What would it mean to NOT walk in your call?

_____

_____

_____

_____

3. Avoid burnout: a) List everything you are currently doing on a sheet of paper. b) Place a checkmark next to everything on your list that the Lord told you to do. c) Stop doing everything without a check.

CHAPTER 9
CHURCH HURT

We have often heard, and we have occasionally repeated, the statement that God is an intentional God, in control of every area of our lives. But do we believe it? No, do we really believe it or is this just something we say when words of comfort are needed for someone else? I love to believe, and quite often remind others, that for every single thing that happens in our lives, God either sent it or He allowed it. Yes, in case you are wondering, I, one hundred percent, believe just that. My God is in control of my life. He has never lost control. God never had anything to sneak up on Him of which He was unaware. There have never been any unintended consequences, for God, as a result of one action taken versus another. And as such, God caused or suffered to be so, everything that happens - has happened and that which will happen, in my life.

Coming to fully embrace this as truth could sometimes be problematic, for our natural selves. The challenge is never with the good things or things we like, these are easy to attribute to our great and loving Father. For example, we know God is at work in the good things like receiving our dream job, having a great and fulfilling marriage, or a marketable skill that we are proud of. We give God praise for receiving unexpected finances, bills paid on time, luxurious vacations, debt cancellation, and nice, reliable transportation. We are thankful for good health, a loving family, and children that are obedient and respectful. Without a doubt we believe that God sent us to a church that teaches good Word, serves as a place of community, and allows us to use our gifts and talents to glorify God. Yes, it is easy for us to say that God led us and is in control of all of these things.

Other events occur that have minimal, even if somewhat troubling, impact on our lives, and these we chalk up, without losing much sleep, to those things that we wonder about. Sometimes, we say we can ask Jesus about them when we see Him face to face - if we still even care. Perhaps we got a good-paying, stable job, but not the one we wanted. We have money to pay our bills but not much left over to do exactly all the things we'd like. Our child was accepted into an excellent college, but not the one we prayed for. The dad that held on, through sickness, for the proposal but transitioned from this life before the actual ceremony. Someone else in the office got the promotion that we thought we should have. Yet, we are grateful because though there was some disappointment, we eventually concede 'that all things work together for our good' and have or will ultimately work out. We hold on knowing our God knows best; we trust Him with our lives, and we grip tightly to that belief.

Then, there are times when we totally forget that God is in control of all things. There is nowhere in all the world, it seems, that people are more put off by disappointment or failed expectations, as they are when it comes to matters in the church. And, when we are disappointed in the church, we are certain that the hurt is of the devil and God had no part in it at all. It's actually quite amazing how quickly we forget that God reigns supreme in all of the universe and yes, even in the structure, hierarchy, building, processes, leadership, and programs of the local church.

Nothing cuts quite as deep as hurt obtained in or from the church. At least this is what the devil tells us and what we readily buy into. There are several problems with Church Hurt, let's look at a few. First is the belief that 'They' just should have known better. Let's define the ambiguous 'They,' as it relates to Church Hurt. 'They' are commonly known as those individuals that may or may not have a known name. They are just They. They could be the pastor or the pastor's wife. They could be the choir director or certain choir members. They could be the usher or the greeters out front. The 'They' could even be visitors that were only passing through. The 'They' could be sourced back to urban legend or something that never actually occurred or misunderstood statements that thanks to the repetitive nature of the story told and retold, now sounds believable but don't even minimally resemble what was.

For sure, 'They' wield lots of power over the minds and actions of the people in the church. 'They,' if you were to believe popular sentiment, are so cunning and skilled that 'They' can elude God and get to the very people that God is trying to love on and mature. However, 'They' do it, 'They' have been hunting people and running them out of the church for many, many years. It is important to note that these same individuals exist in schools, on jobs, in board rooms, in hospitals, and are in many of our customer service jobs. However, when 'They' are operational in these places, the same individuals do not seem to hold the same power.

You see, when 'They' hurt people in the church, 'They' cause others to actually walk out of the building, leave the ministry, and stop attending or worshiping publicly, all together. But, when 'They' cause hurt in any of the other institutions, 'They' no longer have the same ability to cause people to leave. I have yet to see someone hurt or offended in a school and they just walk away with 'School Hurt' and never attend school again. When people are hurt in a retail environment, they don't name it 'Store Hurt' and stop purchasing or buying clothes, matter of fact they call it retail therapy and shop even more. I also see that when people are hurt or offended because of something done on their jobs - 'Work Hurt', they rarely walk away from their job.

I acknowledge that people in the church can and will hurt or offend others. Whether it is done unintentionally or intentionally the pain is real, the disappointment is real, and sometimes there is disbelief or embarrassment coupled with our pain. We somehow expect that once we walk into a religious institution we are insulated from all of the hurts of our past and any hurt that exists in the world. The problem with this thought process is that there are no perfect places, not in the schools, hospitals, boardrooms, work environments, and certainly not in the church. The church is a place made up of imperfect people trying to serve a perfect God. We come through the church doors with all of our own hurts, habits, and hang-ups. We are trying to mature in Christ, we are trying to be more like Jesus, but we are still on a journey and have not yet arrived. Therefore, our issues will cause us to hurt others. We have heard over and over the saying hurt people, hurt people. Until people are healed themselves, they are likely to cause others to be hurt.

I have to also say that sometimes the hurt has nothing to do with the other person or where they are on their journey. Because we ourselves are imperfect people we oftentimes process situations through the sieve of our own unhealthy minds. The problem is internal, but we ascribe the offense to someone or something external. We see what we expect to see, we hear what we expect to hear. If we are coming out of trauma and abuse, as many of us are, we interpret what is going on around us in an unhealthy manner. It is difficult to help someone who sees through flawed lenses; they believe the fractured picture that their eyes are showing them. The sad part is, the individual will run from the church when truly God Himself is the only one that can apply the corrective lenses needed, and with the help and the fellowship of God's people they can gain healthy sight, begin to see their own issues and own up to their mistakes.

God uses people, events, and circumstances to work in us exactly what we need to fulfill our purposes in Him. Yes, we needed the wins in our life. We needed the uncertainties and to learn how to be content and we needed the heartaches and disappointments. Don't run from the good, the bad, or the ugly. There is purpose in pain. In the church, you will experience disappointment or false accusations. Turn your hurt into wonder. "I wonder what this is all about?" I wonder what they are going through that would cause them to act in this manner. I wonder what God is teaching or showing me. What is God preparing me for? Am I being used by God, in a lesson for the other person? Our heart's desire should not be to protect ourselves from any and all hurt but to be yielded to God for His purposes and aware that He has a perfect plan for our life.

God's plans are never for our destruction and are not for our demise. He will use "prickly people" and those that mean well to shape us into a vessel that He can use. And here's an unexpected newsflash, the process hurts. We must understand that not one single thing can be said or done to us that God does not allow. So, if God allowed a thing to happen, it was needed and necessary for the assignment He has for us in this life. I am grateful to God for exposing me to Church Hurt years ago. I know now that it was needed and necessary for the assignment that God had for my life. At the time of this particular incident, I was bewildered, confused, and felt that nothing would ever be the same in church again.

My Church Hurt occurred at the church I was born into. I deeply loved my church, my pastor, and all the people in it. There were about 200 people at the church, and we had a healthy amount of young people in attendance. I was the youth treasurer for the National organization and arranged transportation and hotel accommodations for the congregation twice a year to attend church conventions in Southern California. I sang in the choir and gladly served where needed. I attended church regularly, Bible study, youth groups, and occasionally Sunday School. By this time, though my early twenties, I was married and had one child.

I was totally oblivious to the trouble that was brewing. Serving as the National Youth Treasurer, I worked closely with the National Youth President and National Youth Secretary. We were all young people and worked well together. On a Sunday morning, with my choir robe on, I stood at the cafeteria window to place an order to be picked up, after service. For those that don't know, it was a common occurrence for churches to sell chicken, French fries, ice cream, cakes, cobblers, and sodas to raise money for building projects and to feed the hungry people, after having been in a two-hour service. While standing at the window, one of the ministers spoke, on his way into the sanctuary. I returned the greeting, paid for my order, and also proceeded into the sanctuary and up into the choir stand, using a side door.

Service began with prayer, scripture reading, and congregational singing. The individual that was also serving as the National Youth President happened to be conducting the service. There was a time for people to give during the offering and I heard the service conductor ask for me to come and sing a solo. This was unexpected but not unusual. As I made my way down to the lower pulpit area and took hold of the microphone, the male minister that spoke to me earlier that morning stood abruptly and began to address the audience loudly and somewhat aggressively. I am not certain all of what was said but his speech included his disappointment with favoritism, cliques, what should and should not happen in a church, and … This minister was well respected by the youth and, as far as I was aware, all of us liked him. I remember wondering what had occurred to make him react in this way. I remember thinking, someone has really made him angry. At the end of his speech, I heard him say, "Sit down, Sister Trena"! Confused, I replaced the microphone, not having sung one note, and returned to my seat in the choir stand.

In the stands, other young people seemed just as confused as I was. No one, through the whispering during the continued church service knew what was going on. Someone asked, was he talking about you? I said I didn't think so as I did not know what he was talking about. Someone else wrote a note and wondered why he had me sit down without singing and why this was done in front of the whole congregation. It certainly seemed peculiar. I was embarrassed but thought to myself, I will just ask him after service. This will clear up everything.

I went to the minister not knowing if he would or could divulge the root of what caused him so much consternation, but I expected him to say, this had nothing to do with you. I found and asked the minister what happened, what was that all about? He responded with total vitriol, "You know exactly what you did and I am not playing any games with you!" I was stunned to put it lightly and took a minute to process what he was saying so he, seeing my confusion, repeated that I knew what I had done. I was in shock but managed to ask what he was talking about and what in the world had I done.

Apparently in the short exchange, while I was at the window, the minister asked me to do something on the program. When it was time to do it, I did not get up but when the program conductor (the National Youth President) asked me to sing, I got up to sing. Apparently, in his mind, this was another example of things that were out of alignment in the church, and he was sick of it! I attempted to explain that I did not hear this request and thought he was simply speaking to say Good Morning, but he would not hear it. He basically said I was lying and there was no convincing him otherwise.

Now, I had no previous incidents of trouble, disagreement, or discord with anyone. I was devastated that a simple conversation with clear communication could not solve this issue. It only got worse when I contacted my pastor to see what counsel, comfort, or support he could provide, and he offered none of the above. He didn't necessarily agree with the minister but did not agree with me either nor did he offer to mediate further conversations to bring resolve. Others thought it was a shame but there was no path forward for corrective action - either way.

In absence of resolve, I was embarrassed because he was talking about me, and to this day, I stand on innocence. This was someone I deeply respected so I was tormented in trying to figure out how he got it so wrong. Why would I not do something as simple as what he said he asked? It made absolutely no sense. I was then hurt because of the lack of support from my pastor or any of the other staff or church members, all of whom I had served well. I lost respect for my pastor because, at the time, I felt he was afraid and lacked the courage to question the minister's motives. The hurt moved to offense, then bitterness, and ultimately, I did not want to serve in any capacity at the church! I was hurt in the church, while I attempted to serve God. I wanted to run and not look back.

I love God for ensuring that I did not run. My husband was a musician at the church and so there I sat, stone-faced, in the audience. I determined that though I had to come to church I would not support the pastor, the minister, or agree to anything I heard. I was hurt and no longer trusted or believed anything they had to say! The problem with coming and just sitting is that I was still hearing the word, even if I did not want to receive it.

Over the next several weeks, I could feel God gently massaging my heart. The thought that everything in life will not have an expected and satisfying resolve, kept playing around the edges of my mind. God was lovingly teaching me, way back then, that things will sometimes feel unfinished; everything will not have resolved, yet you have to keep moving. God was showing me that my service unto Him was never about the minister, the pastor, or the conductor of the service. They only did what God allowed them to do. It was needful for me. I had to learn that regardless of what comes into my life, God is still worthy of praise. I do not get to withhold my worship, my time, my tithes, or my love for God's people.

Eventually, amens and other responses began to come out of my mouth. My stone face relaxed and I began to smile a little more each Sunday. Of course, the devil wanted to taunt me by saying they got away with something and that I should be unforgiving because frankly, as far as I know, the minister still thinks I did what he said, so there was no apology ever going to come. Another important and needed lesson, you can forgive and let others off the hook, even if they never ask. Once I released the individuals involved, God begin to fill me with joy and a desire to serve Him, once again to the best of my ability. Church Hurt did not win but it did teach me a valuable and lifelong lesson.

Church Hurt has an element of realness but we cannot let it win. It is only a tool to drive us to where we need to be in God. I have had other Church Hurts in my life but because of that first hurt, God reminds me immediately to put it into proper perspective. I am reminded of the scripture in Matthew 5:10 that says blessed are they that suffer for righteousness sake for theirs is the kingdom of heaven. If your hurt is coming as a result of you acting in righteousness, do not run, rejoice, yours is the kingdom of heaven. If your hurt is coming as a result of something you did, repent, do not run, God is faithful to forgive. Always remember Romans 5:3-5 which paraphrased says we can rejoice when trouble comes because it will ultimately help us. We develop endurance that leads to strength of character that leads to confident hope of salvation that will not disappoint. We will not find a place in the scriptures that tells us to allow Church Hurt or any hurt to cause us to run from church; the place of ministry that you have been placed in.

REFLECTION POINTS

"We can rejoice, too, when we run into problems and trials, for we know that they help us develop endurance. And endurance develops strength of character, and character strengthens our confident hope of salvation. And this hope will not lead to disappointment. For we know how dearly God loves us, because he has given us the Holy Spirit to fill our hearts with his love."

Romans 5:3-5 NLT

1. Evaluate your response the last time you ran into an unwelcome situation. Did you rejoice? The Bible calls it a trial. What verdict would you give yourself?

2. Since you know your problems produce endurance and strength of character, how can you adjust the way you think of your problems?

3. Everything that happens to you in this life is either God sent or God allowed. How should this help you think differently when you run into problems in the church?

CHAPTER 10
FAITH VERSUS COMMON SENSE

Most people take pride in having common sense and sometimes will berate others when they feel common sense has somehow eluded them. When we speak of common sense we think in terms of the practicality of everyday matters in that nearly all people share the same understanding or would behave or respond in the same way. Common sense is an admirable and expected trait though I would contend that perhaps common sense is not, anymore, all that universal or common. Many people, however, still rest on and feel good about their ability to move through life and its demands using their gift of common sense. If you are waiting to see if you have been selected as a new construction worker and 100 people applied, with odds 300:1, common sense would say do not spend money on steel boots, a tool belt, and the required hard hat until they call to confirm the job is yours.

Faith, on the contrary, has no set cadence or rhyme or reason. I hear God saying (through audible voice or some other method) to move so, I am all in, with no evidence or proof. Faith cannot operate solely on your verbal alignment or agreement. You cannot wait until you see movement or for it to begin to make sense to you - not when you are operating in faith. Faith requires that you put action to what you say you believe in - have faith in it and begin to move forward. If God said the job was mine, I start looking for needed supplies; I spend the money now with full belief that the call to accept the job will come at any moment. Faith is the confident expectation, steeped in tangible action, that what I am believing God for is already obtained. It may have never happened before. The odds may be against your choice. It may defy science or nature but based on the promises of God - I shall not be moved by what I see, but only by what I believe.

So how do faith and common sense co-exist? Does faith operate within common sense or despite common sense? Does common sense ever have a faith component? What is your wheelhouse; what are you most comfortable with - operating in common sense or walking in faith? As you begin to think about your answer, what is the evidence of that conclusion in your personal life? What examples come to mind?

When does a true Christ-follower come to grips with reality and make decisions based upon common sense rather than on a "leap of faith" into the unknown, or a "wild shot in the dark", hoping to somehow hit the will of God? I suspect that these questions have long been an enigma for anyone who struggles with walking with the Lord on a day-by-day, moment-by-moment basis. I know it has for me. I found that, if I was not careful and intentional in training my thoughts to operate in the manner in which I desired them to, I ping pong back and forth in my decisions over an issue or response, sometimes in a single day. Until a time came when I was faced with a decision that forced me to take a side and stand in it.

Mid-year as a senior in high school, I was recruited by a major telecommunication company, through a specialized program. Over a weekend, I went from early high-school graduate to full-time employment, with a great salary and amazing benefits. God prospered me over the years; I was blessed with many opportunity assignments and promotions. Before long, I was driving my own company car, frequently traveling throughout the state, and making more money than most individuals I personally knew. I loved my assignments, those that I worked with, and those that worked for me. Over the years, the job provided many challenges and with God's direction, I excelled at each of them.

For a good portion of my career, I ran several Northern California call centers and later moved into a role that included me driving or flying from office to office, basically, teaching mid-level managers how to manage. Right around my 25th service anniversary, though I believed this to be my dream job, I distinctly remember being led or pressed to walk away from the corporate world and serve full-time in the ministry at our church - Victory In Praise. The call or 'God's invitation was to leave the company and utilize the skills gathered over the years, to now teaching leaders how to lead in the kingdom of God. Needless to say, there was no promised salary to accompany the call. There would be no health benefits, stock options, and no company car. Hmmm, work this out using Common Sense or would this be a Faith move?

God gives us intelligence and I believe that His desire is for us to use intelligence with the gifts, skills, and ability He's given, to prosper the kingdom of God and to bring glory to His name. In thinking through the pros and cons of the decision to stay with the company or walk away and serve in full-time ministry, I was conflicted, to say the least. Choosing to stay would allow me continued funds to generously support the ministry. Choosing to leave and work full-time in ministry would leave me with a huge deficit in salary. Common sense told me that I should stay at the company where they loved me and took good care of me, financially. After all, it was God who initially blessed me with the job!

Ultimately and now obvious to some, I chose to operate in faith and trust the prompting of the Holy Spirit. I submitted my resignation letter to my boss and directly to the VP of the company. Though I gave a full thirty days' notice, this unexpected development caused quite a stir within my departments. It felt sudden, it was unforeseen, and my

VP was certain I was either responding to a headhunter - individuals deployed to steal talent from a company by offering better salary, location, or other perks, or had somehow become offended by someone within the company. I turned down offers of increased salary and gave assurances that I was going to work full time in ministry - no one had caused me harm or acted in ill will towards me. I choose God's plan for my life - whatever that plan may entail.

Now, this makes a good story, after the fact, but the challenge is when the sink or swim option is in front of you! What common sense would allow an individual to walk away from a job they loved, healthcare, and financial security? You see, common sense told me that walking away and giving up what I believed to be my dream job was not a good plan, at all! Jobs were hard to come by, especially jobs such as the one I had. Common sense reminded me that I still had children in high school, a mortgage to pay, and fluctuating consistency of incoming tithes from a fairly new ministry.

Where does faith leave off and common sense take over? Or to ask it another way—where does common sense leave off and faith take over? Faith was there repeating, not a promise of what was to come, but just an invitation to trust God and be used in His plans for the ministry. I noticed something. Where Common Sense had a lot to say and, matter of fact, would not be silent concerning her defense, Faith would speak and then stop speaking. When you choose to step out on faith, there will not be a lot of cheers or much sound at all. It's a quiet choice, one of great resolve that requires focus and careful listening to the voice of God. After God initially speaks, if you hear anything at all it will be the lies, tricks, and schemes of the enemy. He wants you to waiver, to cause fear, and to plant seeds of doubt in your decision to move and trust God.

I must admit that way back then I had to put precautions in place to ensure once I took the leap of faith, I was not tempted to go back. It would have only taken one phone call. I was leaving at a time when many influential decision-makers had great love and respect for what

I uniquely brought to the table. Though I fully trusted God, I did not fully trust me. I would not look at old pay stubs and was careful not to encourage callbacks from company associates. My Common Sense mode was still being wrestled into submission to the Faith mode that I wanted to govern my life. I put safeguards all around me to ensure I stood firm in my faith decision. I begin loudly proclaiming to others what God said and why I was leaving. I was blessed to serve and train leaders in the Corporate world; I was now being called to train and serve leaders that are attempting to lead in ministry. This made it harder to later go back and say well, I do not want to serve God's people in the same way.

I am fully aware that most people will still place a high value on the role of common sense in the decision-making process. But what I also now know is, common sense can never hold a candle or compare to the sureness and power of walking in faith. Additionally, where I could not have known it before, would not have seen it before, I now personally know that the God I serve is well able to care for me, the Turner family, and all of VIP, all by Himself. In trusting Jesus, there never was a risk. God did not just start being my Provider in this moment, He was there, providing, all the time.

People can have faith in many things, other people and in themselves. However, when Jesus is the source of your faith, never be tricked into believing common sense should override your faith moves. The Bible encourages us, over and over, to walk by and live by faith. Faith cannot be seen, tracked, or traced. While there is a place and role that common sense can play in our lives, it should never stand in the place of faith in the prompting of Jesus. Operating in uncompromising faith will lift you to places that common sense could never achieve. When offered as a choice, standing on faith over common sense will never disappoint.

REFLECTION POINTS

"Now without faith it is impossible to please God, for the one who draws near to Him must believe that He exists and rewards those who seek Him.
Hebrews 11:6 HCSB

1. What is your typical pathway or process for decision making? Do you lean toward common sense or faith as a decision tool?

2. As a believer, should you ever allow common sense to override your faith-led decisions?

CHAPTER 11
LEST WE OFFEND

"God! For real? This, surely, is more than I can bear. What in the world am I going to do?" My facial expression was smiling, I heard pleasant greetings coming out of my mouth, but my insides were screaming protests to God. This just was not fair or okay on any level. What was really going on here and why was I 'chosen' to be included. Actually, I knew, indeed I did. I knew why I was selected to be in the 'situation' I was in but that knowing certainly did not make it easier at the time.

A couple of years earlier we were blessed to have Frankie join our church family. Though we have a fairly diverse group of families and individuals, Frankie was sent, I am convinced of it, to teach us how to love yet another segment of our community. I was never sure what Frankie's full story was or how he came to become a part of our church family but when he showed up, life as we knew it, was never the same.

Loud, towering, brash, abrasive, opinionated, and a lover of people, especially the girls, the young ones would be an adept description of Frankie. With an intimidating stature and normal societal parameters removed, Frankie was a force to be reckoned with. Each Sunday that he showed up at our Sunday morning services we never knew quite what to expect or how to properly prepare for his arrival.

Frankie was a 'friend' to all who allowed him unhindered roam or conversation. However, anyone that attempted to assist Frankie in proper etiquette, "No, Frankie we don't stare at the girls backsides or down their blouses and make suggestive comments", or help him to understand he could not interrupt service, "Frankie, Pastor is up preaching right now, can I answer your question for you?", was in for a show of aggression coupled with a few words that should not be heard on a church campus.

Because our Bishop is such a lover of all people, he ensured that everyone that came into contact with Frankie understood that until God regulated Frankie's mind and behavior, Frankie would learn at a much slower pace regarding accepted societal norms and church protocol. And learn he did. After some passage of time Frankie had fewer and fewer incidents and even began to occasionally attend Bible study.

Bishop and I loved Frankie and Frankie loved his 'Pastor and Mrs. Turner.' With all of the other things that Frankie was learning about belonging, he noticed that Bishop had assistants or 'armor bearers.' Frankie determined that he would meet Bishop at his car and assist with his belongings. He wanted to carry his brief case and take care of the Bishop. Frankie frequently asked to wash our car or come by to help at the house. We assured Frankie that he was doing a great job at the church and appreciated how much he was growing in his knowledge about Christ.

I received a call at home one day from an unknown number. It was Frankie. Frankie began to explain to me, that he wanted a wife, a wife that was in church. Frankie stated that he had needs and wanted to ask me if it was okay if he masturbated. Yikes! I told Frankie that I was certain God had just the right wife for him, but he should really discuss his sexual needs and desires with the Bishop or one of the other men in the church. At this point, God began to show me Frankie in the light of a younger son. Physically, Frankie was old as or older than me. Mentally however, he was more like 12 to 14.

Frankie continued calling with many relational issues as he attempted to navigate his way through life with the hand he was dealt. One week he would be excited that he found a new girlfriend. The next week he would repent and confess she was a prostitute. He would call hurt because his sure thing girlfriend had him pay her bills and then disappeared. One week he brought a distraught transient woman to my house because he knew that his Pastor could help her with trouble she was having with the county. All in all, many of Frankie's actions and conversations were inappropriate for our accepted standards, but none the less extremely important for Frankie who seemingly had no one else that would assist him in his new desire to do the right things.

One week, Frankie announced that he was ready to get baptized and give his life to Christ. Wow! What an amazing thing. God was working with Frankie, at a pace he could grasp and was leading him to move in closer to Him. A week or so later, Frankie was baptized in a fashion that was true Frankie style. It was loud, celebratory and over the top excitement for everyone. All praises to God!

Sometime after Frankie's baptism we lost contact with him. He stopped coming to church and no one had seen him or knew how to get in contact with him. The truth be told, I am not confident that we extended much effort to find him. Bishop and I were vacationing in Canada, when we started receiving phone calls from relatives of Frankie. They let us know that Frankie had moved to be with them in a different state but was now hospitalized and not expected to live.

Frankie's cousin told us that it took some time for them to track down the right church and pastor, but Frankie was only holding on because he believed that if his Pastor would come and pray for him, he would be healed. Devastated. Bishop explained to the cousin that we were in Canada and not scheduled to be home for another week. He let him know that he would pray now and touch basis when we got home.

Upon our arrival home, we learned that Frankie had passed on. We were heartbroken and had a feeling of great unease. God, should we have left early and flown to be with Frankie? Did we teach Frankie all we could have about You? Did we show Frankie the absolute best love that You have to offer? God responded by letting me know that Frankie wasn't there as much for us to teach him as he was there so that he could teach us.

Indeed, Frankie had taught me a lesson that changed, reshaped my life and way of thinking for ever. It was a test that was special ordered for me, and Frankie was the right one to teach me. My lesson came at a Birthday Picnic. A couple of weeks before Frankie turned 40, he began telling all of the church about his birthday and inviting them to his party. Frankie was so excited and fully expected his church family to show up.

As the day and time for the picnic party rolled around the Bishop and I knew we had to go. We know the scripture 'whatever you do to the least of these' and knew that if nothing else Frankie was a 'least of these.' My grandson was about three at the time and we had him with us. We showed up at the park and an over-the-top excited Frankie came running and screaming, "Pastor Turner, Mrs. Turner!" The grin on his face and light in his eyes said, "I just knew you would come!" Immediately, I was glad we showed up.

The other invited guests all seemed to have Frankie's same or similar 'challenges.' There were only about six of them and each of their faces revealed that they were shocked that Frankie really did have a 'real' pastor that would come to his birthday party. Frankie beamed with pride and everyone else seemed to cease to exist, for him. Only one other member from the church showed up, after some time and for a while, all was good. Then they began to prepare the food for lunch.

Frankie's friends had brought chicken to barbecue on the grill. It was frozen and left sitting in the sun to thaw. It was in its original packaging and had obviously not been pre-cleaned. Because they had prepared the grill, I am assuming, their hands and fingernails were pretty grimy. They opened the chicken and began to place the now partially frozen chicken on the grill. No water, no seasoning, lots of flies. Additionally, they had hot dogs and links to go on the grill. There were a couple of bags of potato chips, (which at this point looked to me like manna from heaven) and deviled eggs. When the container lid came off the eggs, they were beginning to brown from sitting out.

For me, this was a scene straight out of hell. Oh my God, for real! There were no crowds to hide behind, my every action and facial expression was being closely monitored. I smiled, I nodded, I exchanged pleasantries, but inside was a battle raging like none I had ever fought! HELP ME, JESUS!!! What in the world was I going to do? WWJD? Show forth His love and eat what was put before Him. And if it could get any worse, not only was I in this seemingly no way out predicament, but I also had my precious grandson with me. I did not want salmonella, but I absolutely did not want to give it to my toddler grandson!

Oh, I was lost in the terror of my daydreams, someone was talking to me, "What would you like to eat?" Think, think, think. I heard myself respond, "Oh, I would love a hot link and my grandson loves hot dogs." I smiled broader and nodded my head to confirm, yep, that's just what I wanted. "How about some chicken also, we have plenty?", the sweet girl countered. "I better not, but I will take some of those potato chips", I answered. I was keenly aware that God was somehow deriving pleasure from this whole torturous scene. I watched in slow motion as she gladly opened the bag and got our potato chips with her, still grimy, now raw chicken juice added, hands! "Thank you so much", I managed to get out.

A prayer over a meal was never as real for me, as in that moment. "Father God, please bless, sanctify and purify this meal". I wanted to run and hide. Throughout the whole ordeal there was never a question of not eating what was set before me. There would be no way, on this side of heaven that I would offend Frankie and his friends, not for me, not even for my grandson. It is easy to talk about love, but love is action. Love is choosing to take the right action, even when it is not favorable to you. Yes, God was able to purify. He could choose to, or not, but I would not hurt the beautiful people in whose company I was blessed to stand! I looked at Bishop and could tell, mine was a personal war. It was a struggle either he never had or a battle he had fought and won so long ago that he was well beyond this present skirmish. He ate the chicken, the links, the chips, no problem, for him.

We ate, we talked, we laughed, flies buzzed and landed, and I thought to myself, yeah, I am proud of me. Needless to say, we never got sick from our picnic meal. But I did walk away with a lifetime lesson on friendship and esteeming others higher than yourself. The lesson learned, through Frankie has helped me over and over thus far in my life and in many varied settings. At any point I am presented with something that seems beyond what I can deal with or accept, I am reminded of Frankie's Birthday Picnic and know that reflecting Christ's love, is my only option.

REFLECTION POINTS

"The King will reply, 'Truly I tell you, whatever you did for one of the least of these brothers and sisters of mine, you did for me.'
Matthew 25:40 NIV

1. Remove your boundaries: How far are you willing to go to serve those that could be considered 'least'?

2. Heart of a servant: Serving those considered 'the least' is comparable to serving our King. What are the non-negotiable areas in your life, when it comes to serving others, and what is your typical response when pushed in those areas?

CHAPTER 12
DRAINED

My life is truly not my own. This is a statement that most times is said in complete and joyful surrender to God's will in and for my life. There is usually music in the background accompanying the words during praise and worship. However, sometimes it is said in a quiet and tired resolve with perhaps a hint of resentment, "My life is not my own." I can't begin to count the times that I move in what I think is one plan, trip, conversation, event etc.… only to learn that God has a completely different plan.

Most days, this is ok. I sold out a long time ago. Every now and then, this becomes a struggle—of sorts. Not a struggle in that I don't know who is going to win; God always does. It's a struggle because once again I have to remind my flesh, which wants to feel disappointed, let down, forced to move contrary to its will, that you (flesh) are not in control of this vessel. The problem is not so much how you are feeling right now, the flesh always has a set will or desire, but the problem is that I allowed the plan (the flesh's plan) to completely formulate in my mind without heading it off at the path to say, "This temple belongs to the Holy Ghost and will move as He directs!"

Yes, it is almost impossible to begin your day without a thought of what it will entail. Matter of fact, it is a good habit to have a plan or a goal to accomplish every day. When you are sold out for Jesus however, you pray, ask God concerning your day, set out on what you believe to be the best path, and then give God the reigns while keeping your eyes and ears open for detours all along the way, so His will can be accomplished through you!

One Saturday evening, I received a text from a newly acquired friend indicating that his spouse was in the hospital with chest pains. Immediately I knew a few things. First, the person was in the CCU and not ICU, which said to me (my flesh), this is not life or death—let's just pray over the phone. I knew the individual had been harboring un-forgiveness so my second thought was that they should just really seek God for the ability to forgive and all that extra stress and hatred would be removed and therefore the chest pains would possibly be gone. And, because we have an amazing Pastoral Care Ministry, I knew that with one phone call to them the family would be well supported, prayer would go forth, their home would be taken care of, meals for the family would be prepared. However, I knew the individual was so private (or prideful) they would not want anyone else to know and would expect a personal visit from the Bishop and myself.

Man, I was tired, I had two classes to prepare for, I had not yet eaten anything, and limited time left in which to accomplish these things. I love the individual but did not want to have to go! We were in the room about two minutes when the patient on the other side of the curtain called out, "Which ministry are you from?" Bishop went over to respond, and the person went into great detail about their sickness, procedures, and how they got there. She shared how she had been having debilitating migraine headaches and unable to eat or sleep. The doctors were unable to determine a cause or give her total relief. I am thinking, "You have got to be kidding?" It sounded to me like the individual was a believer and for sure knew how to get in touch with the Lord. Where was her people? Where was her pastor? I don't mind praying for other people and frequently do, and she certainly needed a move or even miracle from God. I just wanted her to stop talking so Bishop would pray for her, come back on our side of the curtain, visit and pray for our member, (the person we came to see), so we can go home.

Before I knew it, I was on the other side of the curtain with the very talkative woman. With six degrees of separation, in a short timeframe we learned that I knew her daughter, son-in-law, her grandchildren and many others of the same people. Wow, small, small world.

We spent less than five minutes with the member we came to see; she appreciated the visit and was resting well. Later that night, Bishop received a text stating that the severe headaches that the woman behind the curtain had been having, were totally gone! To God be the glory! When we say we are a willing and open vessel for God to use, we better mean it. And, use us He will, even when we feel we have no more to give!

The following day was Sunday, and as I sat in service, every bit of strength and resolve I mustered up for this brand new day, drained out of my body. I remember wondering if this is what people felt when they have been described as, "She just slipped away"? It is sheer will power that prevents me from sliding like a cartoon character down my chair and onto the floor. That would feel so good, so … right. I don't want service to end, I do not want any attention, I am not in any pain, I have not been mistreated; I am just spent. I am all wrung out. I am all poured out. Empty. That, I think is the best description.

What happened? The first service seemed to go well; there were no telltale signs of this total lack of energy. I want to, at the very least, go home and curl up in my bed. I know to lift my hands; I know to smile and at least mouth the words to the song. I nod my head in agreement with what is going on around me—without me, and I make myself stand at the appropriate times. When it is time to read the word, I do it to the best of my ability. I feel like I am wading through pea soup everything seems to be in a fog.

I make it through the second service but today I am blessed to have to really press my way. There is a third service at 3:00pm that I absolutely must attend. I wonder, to no one in particular, "Is there anyone else that truly believes that they do not have the option of just not showing up?" I truly don't believe there is. Too many times people will say they stayed home because they were just too tired. They stayed because their in-laws came into town. Because their dog had puppies. Because they felt like they were going to be sick. None of those reasons-real or make believe are suitable excuses for me not showing up. This is not because people will not allow it. It is not because my husband will not allow it. It is because I will not allow it. I believe that I am an intricate part of ministry and though I absolutely do not need to be out front, I really do not want to miss anything that God is doing for us. If I want others to support and press in for God, then I am certainly going to support and be the best 'presser-iner' that I can.

The problem with pressing and pressing and pressing, without allowing God to minister to you and refill you through personal worship and prayer, is that you begin operating on fumes. In this state, our thought process is warped, we make mistakes, we say things we never would have said if we took the time to ensure we were filled with God's spirit. I recall a different time, being just in this place of running on fumes, and I shared with my sister how I really did not care for one of the members. He is loud, obnoxious, intrusive, always a drain on Bishop's time and … This is absolutely not my character. I do not and up to this point had not shared such a negative thought about any of the members. My sister was shocked. I think I was just looking for a space to vent and then move on. I will never forget my sister's response that served as the best correction and lesson that I could have ever received. Cheryl stated, "Girl! If you don't like him then I don't like him either! You never say you don't like somebody so if whatever he did made you say that, I definitely don't like him!" I was blown away. I was so sorry and immediately regretted that I shared my feelings out loud.

You see, if Cheryl had quoted me a scripture to lecture me on why we should never speak poorly of our brothers or sisters in Christ, I am pretty certain I would have just thought to myself, if not said aloud, that she just did not experience the same issues and pressure as I did. I would have no doubt had some quick come back. However, her response convicted me so deeply, I have never made that mistake again! What she did, frightened me. I never, never, never want to cause friction or chasm in the body of Christ. I want us to love one another as Christ loves His church. God allowed me to see how quickly and easily I can become a major pawn in the schemes of the devil. I lost that battle but praise God, the lesson learned from it was such a valuable one- a lesson that stays with me today and causes me to watch my words no matter how I feel.

So, back to my Sunday, I got to the third service wondering, God, how in the world will I make it through this service? About thirty minutes in, I went out to the restroom just to breathe and take a break. I took my time and stopped on the way back in the entryway trying to muster up enough strength to go back in. In that short time period (I was gone less than ten minutes) at least six people came out to see what was wrong and where I was. After the last person, I determined that even on the outside of the church I was causing much too much of a spectacle (apparently) and had better immediately get back in my place in service.

I took a deep breath, ask God to please help me, put my trademark smile on my face and went back into the service. In going down the aisle, even my mom was just rising out of her seat. She said, "I was just coming to check on you." I smiled at her and went on down to the front.

The people of God love me so much. I love them so much. The love and attention can sometimes be overwhelming. It is absolutely exhausting to be in the spotlight 24/7. I do not portray God's people as confused and lacking focus on Him. It is just that I realize that when I do something outside of my norm people will notice. I matter. First Ladies, pastors' wives, clergy leaders, ministry leaders, you matter. You cannot lead from a drained or dry place. Too much is at stake. Running on fumes means that in any given moment your perspective will be tainted. Once that happens you will begin to share faulty or poisoned words. Your actions may not be pleasing unto God. Remember, depending how you act other people will also react.

I have learned when I am snappy, easily angered, or frustrated, more times than not, the fault does not lie in what is going on around me.

The fault is in me. I have not taken the time needed to worship or to pray. There is a difference in leading others in worship and in praying for others. Pastor's wives, we must maintain a space and time to worship God alone and to pray and seek God for ourselves. It is in this space that God will fortify us for every assignment that He has for us. We will go in and show up fresh, empowered and able to clearly hear from God and move as He directs. We also must remember that God alone is the Savior and Provider, our husbands can't fill that role and we certainly can't. God always provides for Himself. When we are constantly tired and drained, perhaps we are taking on work and responding to a call that did not come from God.

REFLECTION POINTS

"For I will pour water on the thirsty land, and streams on the dry ground; I will pour my Spirit upon your offspring, and my blessing on your descendants."

Isaiah 44:3 ESV

1. God's Word promises that He will minister to every dry place in your life. So, when you find yourself tired, drained, and feel like you can't go on, who should you turn to? In doing so, what is your expectation?

   _____

   _____

   _____

   _____

2. What is the difference in being drained from ministry and exhausted from a busy time of serving? Are the solutions for both the same?

_____

_____

_____

_____

CHAPTER 13
SOMETIMES GIANTS LOOK LIKE ANTS

I have heard many sermons preached and songs, sung concerning giants in the land. You know, the story where the Israelites were told to go in and possess their promised land. They sent out a scout team of twelve to see what was in store for them. Two of the scouts returned excited, with good reports, but ten of the twelve scouts, came back and all they could focus on were the giants in the land! The ten reflected how they appeared as mere grasshoppers in comparison. Their reports caused the people to draw back and lose heart. The two individuals with the good report were Caleb and Joshua; they stood firm on what God had spoken and declared that they could take the land!

Sermons illustrate that it doesn't matter how big things are, when God is for you, He is more than the whole world against you. God's promises are sure and all we have to do is walk into our promises. We cannot allow the size of an obstacle to block us. Songs remind us that giants must die, the bigger they are the harder they fall. I come away from these empowering messages determined that I too can take the 'land'. Hearing these inspiring words make me want to scream, "Where are the giants? Direct me to one. I can take him!"

Giant-slaying messages are easy to get hyped-up about. Oh, this is stuff that makes great devotionals and preaches well. I could easily create leadership lessons from these passages of scripture, complete with team exercises to corroborate or underscore the main takeaways. I wonder if it is because subconsciously there is a realization that you will, in all likelihood, never meet or see a real giant. Certainly not a literal giant that has squatter's rights over something that belongs to you! So, imagine my amazement when God spoke to me in the midst of an internal battle stating, sometimes giants look like ants.

Out of the sheer providence of God, while still in the throes of our nation's financial crisis and tanked-out housing market, my husband and I was blessed to purchase a beautiful new home. Everything about this purchase and how it came to be - the price, the location, the floor plan, the increased space, the opportunity to (legally) get out of our current property, (that was upside down), all came into alignment. The Bishop was preaching a series on prosperity and God told us that we would play out what He wanted to do for His people.

In the process of purchasing, we ran into the normal challenges and hurdles. We've been blessed to acquire multiple homes, so we were familiar with the various steps and occasional hurdle. After some tough spots, God blessed the sale to finalize. This was really happening and though I believed God, I was not ready for the sale to move at the pace it did. We quickly began packing and making preparations to relocate. We had been in our former home for eighteen years. The property had been one of models when the community was initially built. The house was in excellent condition, with marble floors, custom cabinetry and beautifully landscaped yards; Perhaps we should have anticipated it but we did not give it much thought; the house sold within 24 hours of hitting the market. What a blessing, right?

The day after the sale closed, we went by the new house for one last walk through. The current occupant had a large family and was on the tail end of removing their possessions. Needless to say, the house was in total disarray. We did a quick walk through to hand off remotes etc. and we received last minute instructions and tips from the previous owners. When we got into the car to go back to the current house, I experienced something that I never had before, regret.

As we were backing out of the driveway everything in me wanted to freak out! I felt trapped, boxed in, full of remorse, afraid, and just convinced that this was the worst mistake of my life! Tears began to flow steadily down my eyes. Oh, my word, what was going on? I am not an overly dramatic person and certainly not a crier. All I kept thinking is, "I changed my mind! I do not want this house. I didn't choose this house. This is not mine. I hate it!" I was thinking all of this internally and normally can bring reason to a situation before I allow audible words to my thoughts. But, no this internal feeling was escalating, not receding, and then there were these darn tears. What in the world would I say to Rufus?

Oh, just forget it, with tears, which could not be hid, coursing down my face, I began to say, no, I began to scream, "I hate it!" I remember the words tumbling out with fierceness while thinking, oops, didn't quite plan on saying it like that. At this point, my mind was carefully crafting an appropriate conversation to have concerning this, but my mouth just kept repeating, "I hate it, I hate it, I don't want it. I don't want this house"! Tears still streaming and because I knew I was being ridiculous, I started laughing! Wow! Schizophrenic for real, tears and laughter, okay, but not really. The look of horror on Rufus' face was something etched forever in my memory. My poor husband, fixer of all things Trena, so help him God, was totally befuddled. Yes, I use the word befuddled because later he shared with me that he kept thinking, "Oh God, the house has closed, what do I do?" and there is no better word to describe the look he had. He had no clue about what caused this sudden shift in my behavior.

He attempted to console me, as best he could. I tried to think what was going on with me that made my total joy about this blessing turn into, what felt like a nightmare. And, you will not believe it, but it was the ants. Yes, ants.

In one of the bedrooms in this huge home there were ants in the closet and in trails leading outside of the closet going to and from some unknown place of importance to them. The carpet was dark brown, so it was difficult to clearly see what was going on or why. So that you will see the insanity of the moment, we walked into a 3,500 square foot home with beautiful stone floors, marble counters, crown molding, fireplace, elaborate high ceilings, gorgeous wood railing on the stairs, whirlpool in the master bath, private balcony in the master suite, a huge great room, manicured yard, built in barbecue pit, full top quality swing set … and I wanted out of the deal and was freaking out over ants.

The ants, for me, was more than a deal breaker but also it was the last straw that came before I even knew I was counting straws. You see, on top of all the amazing structural investments that the previous owners placed into the home, was a ton of 'free living' from the beautiful family that was there before us. They knew how to live in the moment and enjoy life, without much thought, it seemed, into any type of cleaning discipline. There were four very active children and their extremely busy and successful parents. There were hidden and forgotten items everywhere, in every nook and cranny. There were smoke stains from an earlier grease fire in the kitchen, toys in the light fixtures, stashed gum under ledgers and countertops, balls in the yard (that we continued to find six months into ownership), candy behind the stove, jewels in the enclosed fireplace-how? Marks and chips on the walls, and equipment stored and forgotten in the garage. Please hear this, the house was and continues to be a blessing to my family. The house had good bones but the (inconsequential) cosmetics of the home needed attention and love.

I believe that I saw all those things, instinctively knew they were cosmetic only, but my subconscious was taking it all in and adding it all up. When the ants came into view, one of the last rooms shown, I think, I crossed some unforeseen limit and was foolishly ready to throw the proverbial baby out with the bath water. Needless to say, we did not try and back out of our blessing. By the way, this bona Fidel blessing also came with generous gifts of one full year paid HOAs and two years of paid Home Warranty service. We moved in and thoroughly cleaned; some things we fixed and others we ultimately chose to live with.

Here's the thing. God was teaching me, illustrating for me, that I cannot be moved by first appearances. As often is the case, the lesson was never just about ants. This lesson had nothing to do with jewels in the sealed fireplace nor was it just about this home. I needed to see that God's promised blessings, anything worth having, is certainly worth working for. In a promised land you will have to displace the giants but it is within your ability to do so. And no matter how big (and sometimes, how small) a problem is, God has already given you the land. I thought I got the lesson, but God wanted to be sure.

A couple of years after transitioning to a new residence, God also took us through a transition at the church. At Victory In Praise, we had outgrown our facility and our Bishop and board led us through the process of locating and purchasing a new property. The entire experience was nothing short of miraculous. From the time the move was announced to the time we moved into our new property was almost three years. During the three-year period, we spent about a year attempting to find a suitable building in the same city. We finally located a property that we were excited about, entered negotiations, qualified, and had all of the required finances. Through a counter offer, we were asked to remove the contingency of the sale of our property. We were excited for the foreword movement and readily removed it. Unbeknownst to us, a different ministry in the area had been watching our property. They later told us that the configuration was perfect for their unique needs. The church sold within one week with a cash offer. Hallelujah!

The following week, we waited for the seller to sign the new verbally agreed upon contract and return the paperwork with their signature. When there was no contact from the seller, my husband reached out to the seller for status. When Bishop spoke to the person that previously asked him to remove the contingency, he was sharply told that his church would no longer sell 'to him.' This was definitely a shift of behavior. Confused, Bishop asked if he or VIP had done anything to offend? Without offering any explanation, the seller responded no, and he, in no certain terms, requested that my husband not call back again.

Shocked and in total disbelief that this happened, Bishop was not certain of what to do next. I remember someone suggesting that we let the ministry that was purchasing from us know that the deal fell through and we could just stay in our building longer. That did not sit well with the Bishop. Walking in integrity, that was never an option, in my husband's mind, to renege on our agreement with the mosque, which purchased our building. We were excited for them. We completed a final cleaning and walkthrough of the property to ensure our building was in good condition for the transfer of ownership. We blessed the new inhabitants with flatscreen televisions and other electronics that they advised would be useful. And, we were now a 600-member church that was homeless. Oh, my.

We had to have known that God was up to something! By the time we reached our date to be out of our property, there was an offer from a local businessman for us to temporarily use his space so we can continue having church service. We were able to place all of our equipment, chairs, and pulpit into his newly renovated space and use his building to continue having service. But here is the miracle, the owner refused any payment for the use of his building. He stated that God had blessed him, and he wanted to be a blessing to our ministry! We continued to look for a suitable property and remained in this businessman's space for eighteen months! During this time, we did not pay rent, electric or water bills, or anything, we did not even buy toilet paper. When God blessed us with our next property, the space was four times larger than what we thought was ours. Elation!

With larger property comes greater responsibilities and much greater price tags. I was keenly aware of the expanded cost on all of the utility bills and because everything was over-sized, anything that required servicing or repair seemed to cost in the tens of thousands of dollars. Help us, Jesus. One day as I was sitting in one of the conference rooms in the new community development center, I stood to walk into the huge commercial kitchen. I had barely taken a few steps when I once again, in my spirit, heard God say, "There will be giants in the land."

It seemed that each time we navigated one hurdle and monetary need, another monetary hurdle would quickly appear on the horizon. Bills or repairs that would typically cost a thousand or less at the previously owned property now came in at 50 thousand and 100 thousand dollars! Our Bishop would often remind us that there was no need to worry about a $100,000 bill, we didn't have ten thousand. If it were to be, God would have to get it done. He reminded us that God always provided for Himself and that this was God's ministry. These were good reminders, that any battle we faced belonged to God. Since He brought us to it, He would take us through it.

There will be giants. Only four words from God but I knew exactly what He was saying to me. I clearly understood the loving message from Him and the tension that flowed from my body in that moment, gave witness to the unacknowledged worries that I was subconsciously harboring. I learned that just because you do not audibly express fear or worry, does not mean that you are not fearful or worried. Externally, I smiled and encouraged others by telling them that God's got us, and I believed it and meant it. However, Father God knew that though I was saying and doing all of the right things and putting on a brave external face, deep down inside the giants were taunting me.

With a simple, four sentenced reminder, God was assuring me that He had already given us the land and though there were giants (previously ants, this time huge bills), He has given us ability to remove, displace or conquer every one of them! I see you giants, but do you see the giant-slayer, operational in me (in us)! The key revelation for me is that when we step into a God-sized promise (land, project, organization), giants had to be there, they were needful and necessary! The giants were placeholders; in place to occupy the land - manage and provide upkeep, until we arrived. Without God at the core of all we do, we could never manage the assignment, we aren't giants. We are only able to displace the giants because of the power of God that is operational in our lives. As I took those few steps into the kitchen area, a weight was lifted, my spirit was emboldened, and I was ready to slay some giants.

REFLECTION POINTS

"This was their report to Moses: "We entered the land you sent us to explore, and it is indeed a bountiful country—a land flowing with milk and honey. Here is the kind of fruit it produces. But the people living there are powerful, and their towns are large and fortified. We even saw giants there, the descendants of Anak!"

Numbers 13:27-28 NLT

1. Giants come in the form of challenges, people, calamity and the like. Where have you seen giants show up in your life?

2. When you see God's promise fulfilled, what do you focus on? The promise or the ants? Have you identified the needful and necessary purposes of the giants in your land?

3. Overcoming a bad report: There are giants in our land, but we serve a God that is greater than any giant. How are you slaying the giants that show up?

_____

_____

_____

_____

CHAPTER 14
IN JUST A FEW HOURS

In just a few hours I will get a frantic call that will forever change the shape of my life. In just a few hours an event will occur that will shake me to the core of my very being. Even if you knew a life-altering, world-shattering event were to occur in the very near future, how do you prepare for it? I would now answer that you prepare by fully embracing every moment, moving as God instructs, and by cherishing each and every moment you have with those around you. Frequently, tell them and show them that you love them.

My husband and I are richly blessed with seven amazing grand-babies; six that are still close enough for me to hug and spoil and one that is now living his best life with Jesus. Mr. Joseph Barnes, IV or as we called him Joey or sometimes J4, was born to our family on December 22, 2016, and was an answered prayer for my son-in-love, Joseph III, and my baby girl Tia. He was our last lump of sugar and perfect in placement, being the seventh child to the family. Joey brought, in his parent's minds, a sense of completion to their home. Joey was the delight of each of his brothers and sisters. Being the baby, he did not want for anything and always had plenty of arms to hold him and minds to decipher what he needed or wanted.

Joey loved to build with his dad, cuddle with his mom, sing, dance, and 'provide direction' for all of his brothers and sisters. He was the youngest but absolutely knew how to hold his own. At two years young, Joey was proud of the fact that he could count, recite his ABCs, and sing, "Who Stole The Cookies From The Cookie Jar? He loved sports, any type of ball or sports equipment, balloons and he loved riding his bikes and his motorcycle. Joey also loved classical music and he was partial to the color green. Joey did not have time for lots of television, but Paw Patrol seemed to always draw his attention! Joey's smile was infectious it would light up the room and make everyone's heart happy.

Though I tried to win Joey's favor and spoil him like my other grandchildren, Joey, much to my dismay, was a man's man and often chose his Papas over the Grannies. One of Joey's favorite pastimes was hanging with Papa Joe at his ranch, helping to take care of the horses and other animals; it was hard to get Joey out of his cowboy boots, his vest and hat. Joey also loved to be in the pulpit with his very own (soundless) microphone trying to help Papa Rufus preach; he wanted those people saved! Perhaps Joey was working on being a preaching cowboy! Joey would 'lay on hands' and pray for his family and other people even before he could talk. Joey had a serious side to his young character; an air about him like he was on assignment or on an important mission. Sometimes it seemed he was just deep in thought. I often wondered what he was thinking about so intensely. In retrospect it seems that perhaps he somehow knew he had much to accomplish in such a short life.

Joey was truly a gift from God. He put smiles on so many people's faces, the way he walked, and the way he spoke by pointing or giving a thumb's up. We loved that he could use his words when he wanted to, and when he spoke his few words usually came out in bursts of energy and excitement as if the words just erupted out of him. On Joey's last Christmas with us we got a kick out of his ingenious idea of decorating his Christmas tree. Rather than hang his bulbs and ornaments low on the tree or all in one place, like his siblings had done, Joey threw his ornaments up high on the tree, and wherever they stuck, there they stayed.

It was in the evening, at the end of a long work week when I received that fateful call. I was alone in my car trying to navigate one last call with my Fund Development Director. On this side of heaven, I will forever hold the moment I clicked over the phone to hear my oldest granddaughter crying and screaming into the phone. I couldn't initially quite make sense of what she was saying or perhaps even then my mind fought not to understand. I knew there was an emergency and I remember willing myself into 'handle business mode.' But what threatened sheer panic and a slip over into uncontrollable anguish was the other sound I could hear in the background. It was my baby, my daughter and she wailed with grief and pain in a way I had never heard. My giving over to panic was no longer an option. I got the details I needed in order to know how to move in the next crucial moments. I could not have prepared me for this, but God had. There had been an accident at home involving my youngest grandson and I sprang into action making the calls and taking immediate steps that were needed.

That night at San Joaquin General Hospital, we waited as close as we could, friends and family filled the waiting room. We prayed sincerely from our hearts. We cried. We prayed more. We even yelled out to God! Please God, please let us bring Joey home whole, nothing broken or missing. We heard what the doctors said concerning him and the extent of his injuries. The doctor's report didn't change our minds about God and all His power. We are people of faith, and we know and believe that what is impossible with man is possible with God! We know that God can do anything, even what could seem impossible! Nothing is too hard or too late for God! We know that God is a present-day miracle worker!

Our church, Victory In Praise, had been on a fast that same week, from Monday to Friday, January 21-25, 2019. Each day, we had fasted from 8am to 8pm and ended each day with collective prayer at the church building from 6:30pm to 8pm. All week we placed our petitions before God and expected miracles, healing, souls to be filled with the Holy Spirit, and for God to revive our souls. That Friday was to be the culmination; our grand finale of the prayer and fasting; a celebration of all God had and was doing in the lives of His people.

We thought for sure that part of the miracle would be that, despite sustained injuries, Joey would come out of the hospital perfect and whole. We waited in hope and faith, in various rooms at the hospital at this point, because people began arriving from far and near. While waiting, we received a report that Joey was finally stable enough to leave by helicopter to go to UC Davis trauma unit for the extensive treatment that his injuries required. We were all planning to follow him to UC Davis by caravan, so we could meet him there. Soon after those announced plans it became clear that God had a better plan for our Joey! He did leave, not by helicopter, but he left happy and whole from this life! On Friday, January 25th, 2019, Joey's smile grew even brighter as he met the eyes of Jesus in his new forever home in heaven.

The reality and finality of God's plan struck hard. We were required to recall and desperately cling to every scripture, every Word that we had ever read and received! We had to truly release our will to God's will and yield to Him! God, how could anyone endure such an unimaginable loss? How does one prepare for anything like this? Certainly not expectantly or willingly. Is there such a preparation?

Now, we are understanding that during our time of fasting and praying, God was setting up our hearts and minds to take the giant pain and surprise that God's YES, was to transition our Joey, His Joey, at two years of age, to his new perfect forever home! God loved our family so much that He masterfully had our entire church body pray for what was to come. In advance, God covered us, my children and my children's children. In other words, Joey's entire family was fortified for this unexpected and heart-wrenching decision that God had made. Though there are still understandable struggles that we all have, especially Joey's mom, dad and siblings, the continued prayers of the righteous will continue to heal and fortify us to fight and hold on to God, as our faithful and loving God.

We cannot know the future, we cannot know how to plan for the unforeseen, but God knows our future and He has the grace, and strength to fortify us with just what we need.

REFLECTION POINTS

"Your eyes have seen my unformed substance; And in Your book were all written The days that were appointed for me, When as yet there was not one of them [even taking shape]."

Psalms 139:16 AMP

1. God has a perfect plan for your life and He knows, how long He has preordained for you to be here. Still, we hurt and grieve when we lose those we love. What scriptures can you study and cling to, to help through the process of loss?

2. How does your trust in God anchor your faith in Him, when His answer to your petition is different than what you were hoping for?

CHAPTER 15
GOD'S WORD STANDS

The Bishop and I had recently conducted a mini-series on relationships at the church. When a word goes out over the pulpit it will first impact the lives of those sharing the word and then permeate throughout the room touching various lives in whatever state they are in. Your job is to deliver the word, just as God gives it. Giving all honor to God, many individuals and couples reported that they were blessed and encouraged through the word and transparent examples. I came across an email today from one of the couples where the wife was particularly encouraged to hold on in her marriage despite the many challenges she faces. I read the article and was overcome by a sense of sheer dread. I remembered her husband from various counseling sessions. Oh my God! I think her husband is indeed crazy! I think the right thing for her to do is to run, and never look back!

What do you do, when you know more than outward appearances would ordinarily allow you to know? How do you keep your own thoughts, opinions, perspectives, and guidance on 'lock-down' so that only the word of God can speak? This male individual was mentally and physically abusive, manipulative, and, I believe, somewhat delusional. And now the wife was encouraged, through the message that we brought, (yikes) to stand with her husband—through the good and the bad. God??? This can be a setting for a miraculous move of God or a set up for the devil to wreak havoc and have it all garishly splashed across the headlines of the news.

God alone knows the plans that He has for our lives. Every situation that He allows us to go through was carefully crafted for the utmost kingdom impact! All souls are mines declares the Lord. But the soul that sins will surely die. It is easy for us to begin to look at things from a natural perspective. It seemed to me that the person that was in danger of death was the devoted wife that has just gained a renewed determination to hang on in there.

The actual truth of the matter is that the wife was beautifully saved. The truth was if and since God sent that Word that encouraged her to remain with her abusive husband in a volatile relationship that even if she left this life, through the hands of her husband, her life and obedience to the Word would not be in vain. There would be purpose in it, even if we never get to know it. She would have held on to what God told her, even in the face of death, and God will reward her accordingly.

I anticipate getting many attack letters because of this writing. I almost removed it because of the negative reactions I know it will bring. "How can you encourage a person to remain in an abusive relationship?!" However, the truth remains is that we will all leave this life one way or another. Whichever way God chooses for us to transition into the next life, we pray that it is as result of our being fully yielded to Him.

I do not condone violence against women, men, children, or animals. I do believe that God, not only spoke divine words that inspired scripture, but He also continues to speak to His people today. I believe that God is fully aware of and still divinely sends His Word over the pulpit in full knowledge of who will hear it and receive direction for their lives. This is not me listening to a situation and feeling a certain way about what should happen. God sent His Word, the messenger delivered it, and the receiver embraced the Word that gave direction to their next steps.

When we feel like we love people better than God, we are tempted to jump in and say, "Well, your situation is different. Perhaps you should still …" I was definitely tempted to 'help' this beautiful woman of God by suggesting that the Word may not have been for her or that perhaps she drew the wrong conclusion. I could sense the spirit of God telling me to hold my tongue about my thoughts and to be still. No matter what the outcome, God's Word stands alone. "Ok", I heard myself say, "All glory to God".

God alone is God. He has a perfect plan for our lives. A perfect plan, according to His will and His purposes. This particular young lady eventually moved away. We did not get to see how God moved or know the outcome of their lives. Was the husband saved because of his wife's witness? Is she still holding on to the promises of God and waiting for them to come to fruition? Is she in heaven in the presence of God, having served God in her time? Only God knows.

My prayer is that whether on this side or in life eternal, she never let go of God's Word. We do not get to receive God's Word for our lives when it is in alignment with what we want to hear and then reject it and do our own thing when we don't like what He is saying to us. Of course, the devil always wants us to only see what we perceive to be the downside of obedience to a less that favorable directive.

We reason and 'common sense' ourselves into being disobedient to God. God wants me to be happy, we say. I do not have to take this, we say. Nobody should live like this, we say. If you are in right relationship with God, the bible promises that you have the Greater One living in you. Here's a thought. Do we really believe that whatever it is we are going through is because of God a) not caring, b) not watching, c) incapable of moving, or d)???

God's Word is full of promises to the believer and every one of His promises are yes and amen. So, if and since you may indeed be suffering through some sort of injustice or mistreatment in your relationship, just know this, the plan that God has for your life is greater than the pain you are enduring. In the Old Testament, Joseph suffered many hard trials in order to save a nation. It is difficult to see any good that can come from pain and heartache, in the middle of suffering. Yet, God's

Word stands. If you are suffering for Christ's sake, the Bible promises rewards for your labor. He is using you for His glory. Hold on to God's Word, no matter what. Not one tear or hurt will be wasted, God loves you and He always has a plan. Through your testimony of hearing and standing on God's Word you too may save nations.

Quick note: If you are suffering in a relationship outside of God's will, this word is not for you. Seek God for salvation and direction concerning your life. Ask God to break every unbiblical soul tie and to order your steps concerning His will for your life.

REFLECTION POINTS

"For all the promises of God in Him are Yes, and in Him Amen, to the glory of God through us."
2 Corinthians 1:20 NKJV

"As for you, what you intended against me for evil, God intended for good, in order to accomplish a day like this—to preserve the lives of many people. ."
Genesis 50:20 BSB

1. In order to know God's will for your life, you must first know God. Take some time daily to study the character of God and seek Him for clarity of instruction and direction.

CHAPTER 16

MY HOPE IS BUILT ON NOTHING LESS

My hope is built on nothing less than Jesus' blood and righteousness. I cannot hope in people; their promises, intentions, well meaning, good thoughts etc. - people will not only let you down, they will step on you, stomp on you, grind you under their feet and then back over you like they were performing a mere Moonwalk, in the style of Michael Jackson or Fred Astaire. Jesus you are Lord! You alone rest rule and abide in my life. Every one of your promises are yes and amen. You are not a God that can or will lie. You perform every one of your words. You are a promise keeper. Yes, God, I can hope in you, a hope that needs not be ashamed. But, oh God, Your people....

I stopped counting the number of times I poured into and supported people only to have them act like I should have. We've paid car notes, electric bills, helped with rent, supplied emergency cash, and God knows what else. I told myself that I was glad to provide the finances because this was a way to minister to their immediate need. My hope was they would be grateful and therefore serve God more faithfully at VIP. I want you to know, it rarely works out this way. People develop amnesia and when you need them to serve in some capacity they are frequently nowhere to be found.

How many times will I let people continue to set me up for failure? How many times will I allow them to push me out on a ledge only to have them saw off the entire branch? Levels of devastation - yes, when I mean no. No, when I mean no and contrary to all your efforts poured into me, I am not trying to say yes. Promises to support that never come to fruition. Now that you use all of your resources for you, waste resources for them, and now pay out additional resources because they were a no show. Only to come home and still be further 'got' because you didn't even do what you should have done while you stayed home. Then you have those that are exercising faith that show up with none of their own finances, so you get to also support them, while already out on a frail limb.

Devastation comes because I built my hope on their word and not Your Word. I am the problem, God, help me to fix me. I want my hope to be only in You. I was never called to help people or give them finances as a trade off for their loyalty. I learned to help through counsel, prayer, love and to help with finances, when sowing into good ground and as God instructs me to do so. When we correct our expectation, we are not so easily disappointed or devastated in broken promises. People are just people. Most of the time they mean well but they are also under attack. The enemy does not want them to fulfill their purposes in ministry and if they can distract you in the process, that's a bonus win for the devil.

I am reminded a scene that played out in one of the stories recounted in the gospels. Earlier in the evening, Jesus foretold of his pending death and revealed to His disciples that they would later betray and desert Him. Peter vehemently assured Jesus that he could count on him that he would never betray him. Peter meant well and at the time Peter spoke it, he meant every word that he forcefully declared. Jesus, though He poured into Peter as one of His core disciples, knew differently. After Jesus was betrayed and arrested, we next read that Peter is found warming himself by the fire, at the palace of the high priest, having deserted Jesus, just like Jesus said he would. Furthermore, Peter denied

Jesus, just as strong as he stated that he would not. He now vehemently declared that he did not know Jesus! And, of course, the rooster crowed and reminded him of Jesus' words.

Was Jesus distracted by devastation that His disciples did not stick with Him or that Peter did not keep his word? I submit not. He knew His eleven disciples meant well and Jesus knew the challenges that they faced in their flesh. They were still growing in their faith and had much to learn. Peter wanted to be with Jesus which is why he didn't run in a completely different direction. But when it was time for Peter to speak up and bear witness to who Jesus was in his life he choked - lied. Jesus felt compassion for Peter in that moment and at the same time Jesus did not lose any ground in accomplishing His assignment.

God, help me to look on people with compassion when they 'choke,' are fearful, forgetful, or just do not show up. They, too, are growing in their faith and in their maturity. Peter went on, despite his setback, to receive special revelation from Jesus and was given the Keys to the Kingdom. Would Peter ever have had the ability to achieve this status had Jesus openly berated him or wrote him off as not dependable and unworthy of another chance?

I want to see people like Jesus does. My husband easily sees people 'in their future' and not as they are in their present state. I fully believe that Jesus sees our end and is aware of the many missteps that we will take in getting there. My hope is built on nothing less than Jesus' blood and righteousness. The blood that Jesus shared as He carried out His foretold death has the power to cover all of my faults and it has the power to cover others. Hope, like faith, continually looks forward and expects the best in people and in situations. What I have learned and what I witness on a regular basis is that if you expect the best of people, they usually come with their best game. When you are skeptical and express distrust it becomes sort of a self-fulfilling prophecy and people show up, based on what you called forth.

I want to love like Jesus loves and lean on Him to empower His people to show up, grow up, and shine in Him. Since asking God to shift my mental attitude and fix my heart, like a magnet, I attract people that want to serve to the best of their ability. People do not want to disappoint. I cannot even imagine Peter's sorrow when he knew that Jesus knew of his failure. The gospel lets us know at one point that their eyes briefly met, and that Peter wept bitterly. When people fail, I am now quick to remind them that any failure that they may experience is not permanent and it does not and will not define who they are - not in my eyes, and certainly not in God's eyes. I appreciate them for what their desire was, encourage them to plan better for the future, remind them that they are a work in progress - keep moving forward and determine that on their next attempt, their efforts will be successful.

This shift, in me, gives me something different to focus on. I no longer focus on pass or fail, delivered on the promise, or dropped the ball. Now, I spend time partnering with the work of Christ and in encouraging people on their journey to receive revelation from Jesus and their own type of Keys to the Kingdom. Any role that I can play in encouraging more Peters to continue on their growth to maturity is counted, not as a devastation but as a blessing and as an honor.

REFLECTION POINTS

"Let us hold unswervingly to the hope we profess, for he who promised is faithful.

Hebrews 10:23 NIV

"May your unfailing love be with us, LORD, even as we put our hope in you.

Psalms 33:22 NIV

1. God is faithful, people may or may not be. How can you right-size your expectation of others, so that you are always able to love them, in spite of their performance?

2. Make a list of anyone in your past that you may have 'written off' because of a perceived failure. Say a prayer for each of them that God will use them for great works in the Kingdom.

CHAPTER 17
ATTACKS

When you are intimate with a person you want the very best for them. You never want them to be mistreated and you always want to make sure that in anything they attempt, their best foot is placed forward. God is indeed our protector and keeper but one of my greatest challenges comes in when I feel like the Bishop is under attack.

My Bishop is a caring, patient, and kind individual. Bishop loves God, for real, at home as well as at the church. He is consistent in his words and actions concerning his spiritual walk. What he teaches and preaches in the pulpit is what he exemplifies at home, on vacation, with his family, and with his friends. He loves all people regardless of age or race. The Bishop genuinely wants to see people grow spiritually and naturally. I do not know what it would be like, and for sure it would make for a very different story if the Bishop did not live as he preached, but he does. And, since he lives all he knows how for God, and therefore does all he can for God's people, I have a problem when people mistreat him!

Outside of this arrangement that I have, sleeping with the Bishop, it would be quite the norm to strike back when someone lashes out or sets up traps for your man. For certain, it would be understood, especially if there was an effort made to 'mature in the Lord' and allow God to fight your battles. However, in my role, I intrinsically know that it is never the right response to retaliate for any of the schemes set up by and through 'church folk.' The 'key man' will take hits. There will be attacks. The devil will try to discredit, discourage, disgrace, devastate, and deceive through lies, lust, lack, and longing, and will use any one to accomplish it. People will never cease to shock you. Just when you think you really know someone, they will do something devastating that will negatively impact you.

God does not allow you to uncover or expose your attacker. You get to continue loving them, speaking the Word to them, and coming to their rescue as God sends you out to do His bidding. He requires that you pray for them (that despitefully use you) and pray that they will be blessed (and sometimes they are). And, sometimes, there is the promised vengeance that God alone gets to mete out.

Years back, there was a young woman and her husband in our congregation. The husband had some spiritual background and upbringing, but his wife had some lived street experience and was new to the faith and trying to work out her own path in this new call on her life. We were pulling for and praying for her as, like many others, this was a new experience for her. She eventually became a good example of a person that stays around church too long without allowing God to truly do a work in their life. I think it tragic that people will believe that they have to 'act' holy or Christian without ever coming into the realization that Jesus is who He says He is and has ability to totally transform lives when you confess, repent, and accept Him into your life as Lord and Savior. Unfortunately, as suspected, this young wife played the role but did not truly submit to God and trust Him to make her new in Christ. She said all the right things, she did many of the right things, but again time would prove, that it was mostly surface sentiment.

Because of her skills and natural talents, after the passage of some time, she desired to serve in ministry. She was given the opportunity to take an administrative leadership role in the church. Eventually, because there was lack of follow through and commitment, she was moved from the given volunteer position. The young woman, that we shall call Kay, stated in the meeting that was called to transition her out of the position, that she understood and agreed with the decision. Internally, and unbeknownst to us, she was livid.

Leaving that space, Kay determined that she would make the pastor (and I) pay, for degrading her by taking this position. We had no clue that this was a 'thing,' and that people would be vindictive to this extent or level. Kay went about concocting an elaborate plan to expose one of our children to cocaine. According to her later confession, she intentionally tried to get our child hooked on narcotics. Not knowing any of this was going on, there was conflict in our home, clashes between our son and my husband and eventually a blow up that led to words shared and a fracture in our home.

Kay began or increased using (drugs) and loss lots of weight. She bragged to the naive and unsuspecting church members and to anyone that would listen, that she was on a new health regimen. She agreed to 'help' some of them with their weight loss journey through her tips on diet and exercise. I could only see her, at this point, for the manipulating individual that she was. I recalled several conversations of the past and though there was always this nagging unease, I overrode it as her just being a different and unique individual. At this point, I was angry and day by day was less and less willing to control my actions. I was angry, as she was expertly sowing seeds of discord in the ministry and spreading lies that I could now clearly see through, all the while gloating in my discomfort. Even at this point, I did not know the full picture and had no idea the intentionality and severity of her actions.

At some point I decided that I was going to tell her off and give her the 'whipping' that she was begging for. I said to no one but myself, that the very next time, Kay approached me, I was going to beat her tail! I believe it was mid-week when I made this assertion. On the very next Saturday, God Himself intervened.

Every Saturday, during this time we held a small Bible study discussion in our home called Small Group. There would typically be 12 to 15 people gathered in our upstairs Great Room. At the inclusion of Saturday's Small Group, one of the ladies lingered behind. This particular woman was an individual that had spent a lot of time 'in the street life and life in turn had not been particularly kind to her. She was sweet and sincere but was sometimes challenged with comprehension. She had a particular fondness for me and almost, without fail, since the time she became a part of our ministry would tell me, every time she saw me, "Ooh, First Lady, you so pretty!"

At the conclusion of Small Group that Saturday, as couples and individuals went downstairs to leave this lady, Ms. Glenda, (not her name, obviously) lingered behind. I could tell that she wanted to say something but was very hesitant to say it. In all the times that she addressed me, she always said the same thing. This Saturday however, when she gained the confidence to speak, she started the same, "Ooh, First Lady, you so pretty." But what she said next totally stunned me. She continued, "Don't ever let anybody make you act ugly." I stared at her, shocked but not confused! My failure to respond made her feel she had offended me, and she began stuttering but repeating the same thing, but this time ran all together, "First Lady, you so pretty but don't ever let anybody make you act ugly."

Oh, my word. I let her know I appreciated her for sharing her words. I knew though, that they were words that came straight from the mouth of God! Though I had not told a single solitary soul of my plans, not even my husband, and I had acted in no way foul, up to this point, against Kay, God knew my intentions. I was blown away by God's love and humbled by his correction. The randomness that God would use a soul such as Ms. Glenda, not one of the staff or other leaders to stop me in my tracks, was just masterful.

On that Sunday morning, almost to see if he (the devil) could chide me into going back on my renewed commitment to follow peace with all men (and women), rather than avoid me or me having to approach her, the devil had Kay (yes, I believe the devil prompted her), to approach me as soon as she saw me Sunday morning. With her voice dripping with honey and delight, Kay let me know that she was in a particular step of her recovery program that required her to confess to those that she had wronged. As she was enjoying every minute of the setup she proceeded to tell me that she had intentionally exposed my teenaged son to cocaine and wanted to give me every other detail of her other misdeeds. The Holy Spirit quietly spoke to me and said quickly forgive her. I interrupted Kay as she prepared to elaborate and say, "I forgive you." She looked dazed and confused. Her plan was to relish in all of the sordid details to further cause me pain and discomfort, under the guise of making amends. I heard her say, "But, I need to share with you what I did to move forward in my steps." Once again, I told her I forgave her and there was no need for her to share all the details. She looked as if all of the air was released from her balloon; she sat, totally deflated. I thanked her and got up leaving her in the seat.

I am encouraged in the fact that God is still working out His perfect work in my children and He is still crafting the testimony for both of their lives. As for me, God alone helped me to come out of that attack with my testimony intact. There is no way that I should ever had needed God to intervene in my pending actions. I knew better! I should have had enough Word in me and around me, with enough upbringing and teaching in the church, that I should have seen exactly who was at work. I should have recognized the spiritual warfare that was being waged and my determination and plans should have been in how to fight in the spirit.

The devil knows how important legacy is and he sought to destroy by attacking what was near and dear to my husband, his family. Any attack against God's people, even my husband and family, was not my battle to fight in the flesh. God said touch not my anointed; His chosen people, and do my prophet no harm and the Bible tells us that vengeance belongs solely to God. I repented and had a renewed determination to serve God and not be ensnared by the devil. I shudder to think of the damage I would have caused to the testimony of our ministry and to the body of Christ. I am still grateful to God for redirecting my steps.

As for Ms. Kay, it wasn't too long after that, at a still young age, she encountered tragedy and was found deceased. God's Word stands sure. Be careful how you treat God's people - all of them. My very actions could have placed me on the side of those that attack God's people for in the Word of God, God declares that all souls are His, but the soul that sins will surely die. I learned to pray for people that mistreat you and despitefully use you. People think they are getting away with attacking God's people, but the truth of the matter is no one can afford to be on the wrong side of an angry God.

REFLECTION POINTS

"Yet he did not let anyone oppress them. He warned kings on their behalf: "Do not touch my chosen people, and do not hurt my prophets."
1 Chronicles 16:21-22

"Beloved, never avenge yourselves, but leave it to the wrath of God, for it is written, "Vengeance is mine, I will repay, says the Lord."
Romans 12:19 ESV

1. Describe a time when you possibly interfered with God's plan, by standing up for your believed rights?

_____

_____

_____

_____

2. Can God trust you to allow Him to handle sensitive affairs in your life? What is the evidence of your response, whether He can or cannot?

CHAPTER 18
I GET TO WORSHIP

In prayer this morning I was reminded about what an awesome privilege it is to belong to God. How can it even be put into words? God chose me to serve Him. What an honor it is to serve the risen Savior? This was huge, as I felt God lovingly reminding me that I 'get' to worship Him. Only days earlier I allowed the enemy to dampen my spirits and was feeling overwhelmed by the 'burden' of ministry. Because God is so faithful, He sent a reminder word through a message of sowing into others. You can bet I was straight after that. I felt like the commercial when the person slaps himself upside the head exclaiming, "I should've had a V8!" I tell you during that time I certainly was not thinking of the blessing it was that I get to know who Jesus is. And, isn't that the way it is when we feel over-loaded. In my experience, the problem has never been that God put too much on me. The issue is always the same, once I realize it, at some point, I forgot to let God be in control. Usually, I have taken my focus off God and His ability to do great and mighty works. He even uses me to accomplish some of the great works and then I get crazy and think it was me, and then God lets me get a taste of what it would be like if it was me, and then I get overwhelmed and even crazier, and … You know the pattern. So, thank God, I am back on track.

So, in the presence of God, I was moved to tears by His greatness and the vastness of His love for His people. Wow, what an amazing God we serve. While in prayer, the second great thing that God did on this day was to place two ladies in my spirit. I immediately recognized a similarity in their situations in that they were both going through extremely hard times. Their struggles, though very different circumstances had both continued for over a long period of time. Therefore, I immediately begin praying for strength, endurance, patience, and long-suffering. God then let me know that His strength had been made perfect in their weakness. That even in their worst times, in their darkest days, they brought glory to Him. He was well pleased with their undying loyalty and service unto Him. They were indeed both sold out to Him. The song that came to mind, "And, they shall be mines, said the Lord." Wow, what are you showing me, God? God replied, "This is what real love is all about. They do not love me because their situations are fixed. They do not love or serve me because they have an inside view that things will turn out all right. They serve me nevertheless! Despite! They are determined to love me, no matter what the outcome of their lives."

God let me know that He showed me the two ladies as lifted examples. He stated that it was because I need to pray for the entire Body of Christ, that love increases and that the Body would come into the full knowledge of why they live for me and love me. Real love cannot be situational. Real love cannot be 'dependent on.' Real love cannot be circumstantial. Times are not always hard. Life does not always hurt and disappoint. However, when it is and when it does, God's people have got to know that they are living this life to reflect the glory and goodness of Christ. And God's goodness is not shaken or changed based on external occurrences. God's goodness will allow or let the external occurrences cause the inner glory to shine even brighter when pressed.

It is so time to move beyond the 'I am barely hanging on and I want everyone to know it' stages in our lives. God is faithful and He is a good God, all of the time. Everything that happens in our lives God either sent it or allowed it to be. Yes, it is easy and a natural response to worship out of abundance and when we are showered with the good things in life. We worship when our children are all well and when prayers are positively answered.

At some point, beautiful people of God, we simply must progress and mature from loving on the Lord only when we like what is going on in our lives. For those that are going through struggles, right now, you already know the greatness of God. You know that He is a miracle worker. You know that God is in control and has never lost control. You also know that God suffers some things to come to pass and it is all for our good. The Bible calls them light afflictions and reminds us that what we suffer now is nothing compared to the glory he will give us later.

When we first began our ministry, years ago, God let me see a pattern in me. I gave my best worship at church while things were going well. I was moody and withdrawn at church when presented with life's challenges. Soon, I taught the devil that he could impact my praise just by causing negative situations to occur prior to church services. Thank God, the ministry was small in size because I, in turn, was teaching the people, by my actions, the same thing.

God's Spirit is real and will speak to you if you will listen. The Spirit of God began to show me the tantrums I was throwing when things didn't go my way. In love, He showed me that there are certain things that I absolutely had to go through if I was going to grow and if I was willing to let Him receive glory through my life. Romans 8:28 began to come alive for me in its true meaning. If I understood that all things were working together for good to them that love God and were called for His purpose, I would then also understand that whatever was going on in my life was either working something out in me, for me, or for someone else that also loves the Lord. Hmmm, this thing may not even be about me!

I began to see that if I would let the devil block my praise, not just at church but also in my life, I not only missed opportunities for God to bless me and do miraculous things in my life, but I also missed opportunities for God to use me to show His greatness to others. By consistently worshipping God regardless of what was going on in my life I then begin to live the Word, I will bless the Lord at all times and His praise shall continually be in my mouth! I embodied the scripture that asks, "What shall separate me from the love of God?" It certainly does not mean that God does not love us if we are hungry or cold or in trouble or sick! It means that God knows my love for Him and my worship is not situational and bad times will not stop my praise.

God, I worship you because you are always worthy of worship. It is a privilege to know you and to serve you. You are good and you are good - all the time! My worship is no longer contingent upon circumstances or how I feel. My worship is a choice that I make daily. No, I do not have to worship you, I get to worship you, and I get to worship, in spite of …

REFLECTION POINTS

"Come let us worship and bow down. Let us kneel before the Lord our maker, for He is our God.

Psalm 95:6

"Who may worship in your sanctuary, Lord? Who may enter your presence on your holy hill? Those who lead blameless lives and do what is right, speaking the truth from sincere hearts."

Psalm 15:1-2

"Even though the fig trees have no blossoms, and there are no grapes on the vines; even though the olive crop fails, and the fields lie empty and barren; even though the flocks die in the fields, and the cattle barns are empty, yet I will rejoice in the Lord! I will be joyful in the God of my salvation!"

Habakkuk 3:17-18 KJV

1. Consider taking some time, now, to steal away to a quiet place and worship God, just because He is a good and worthy God. Do it, just because you get to.

   _____

   _____

   _____

   _____

CHAPTER 19
DANGERS SEEN AND UNSEEN

Growing up at my childhood church in Richmond, CA, our pastor, Bishop Albert Lee Jackson, would always pray the same consistent prayer as a benediction. Though we could recite it, in jest, as kids, I can now only remember it in part. "… protect and keep us from dangers seen and unseen, as we leave this place but never from Your presence, bless us over the dangerous highways, freeways and streets, even in our homes. Enable us to keep looking up, looking up to thee …" Only as an adult, fully aware of the many dangers lurking around every corner and with the internet, 'even in our homes', resonates more and more and I now fully appreciate the prayer covering our Bishop released over us, service after service.

On one of our anniversary getaways, Rufus and I pulled into our resort, the Jewel Paradise Beach and Spa, in Jamaica. We were let out in front, as our driver transferred our bags to the porter and drove away. It was only after the transport driver left that it was determined that our reservations were actually made at their sister property up the road. No problem 'Mon', yes indeed, we were back in Jamaica.

The front desk receptionist arranged for one of the bellmen to pull a car around (it appeared as if it was a personal vehicle) and drop us up the road. Now, upon approaching the second property in an unauthorized vehicle the security at the front gate was on high alert. He needed the driver's name and plate number. Security needed our names and needed to know why the driver was transporting us. Our driver explained. After checking and rechecking, security radioed ahead and allowed us entrance.

Our check-in process was quick and uneventful. We were shown to our room by the bellman with our bags in tow. The property was nice, well appointed, clean, the people well trained, courteous, and the weather gorgeous. After a few days, however, there were a few things that stood out as not the norm for our travel experience.

Out on the pristine private beach there was a security guard inconspicuously posted at each ending point of the property. On the walkways posted among the beautiful and lavishly appointed gardens were other armed guards, sprinkled here and there. As we took tours off and returned to the property whether by land or sea, you guessed it, if you paid attention and looked carefully, you were constantly under the watchful gaze of one or two security guards.

The resort was very nice and offered turn down room services and kept the mini bars filled with your personal preference of drinks daily. On the days or evenings that we happened to be in the room, we noticed that each time a person came to stock our room they had security with them. Now this was getting just plain weird. On our late-night walks on the pier, on our strolls to the gardens or spa, there they were at least one security patrol.

The resort staff was all very engaging, full of smiles, tips, suggestions for tours or meal choices. The resort staff made a point of learning and remembering our names; they asked concerning our stay to ensure we were having a great time and would return. I asked Troy concerning the Jerk Chicken and he hand wrote the recipe for me and brought it to me the next night to dinner. Sean knew that we enjoyed the Brown Chicken Stew so on his off time he picked up 'browning' from his local neighborhood store that he said I would need when I got back home. Very accommodating and eager to please, each of the resort staff members had pleasant and friendly personalities.

The security's personality stood in stark contrast to the resort staff. They made it clear that we are not here to be your friend, we are not here to entertain you, and we will not be distracted or disarmed by you. Male and female alike, they were there on business. It was evident from their posturing and positioning that though we could not see or feel it, there was a very real and present danger that they were determined to guard against.

Our Bishop's prayer rang out loud and clear from the distant past, "Lord, protect us from dangers seen and unseen." I tried looking around again to see what they saw, to see what could keep them day after day on such a sense of high alert. Nothing. I recalled a few days earlier while booking tours, we asked the lady at the tour desk about venturing out to mingle with the local people. She smiled, shook her head ever so slightly from side to side, and continued signing us up for the approved tours.

Should we be concerned, should we fear, should we be hyper-vigilant and begin to watch for impending danger? We were not led to do so. God let us know that though we were in what could be dangerous territory, we were not only covered by those that believed they were guarding us but we were also covered by the prayers of the saints - our prayers and the many people of God back home praying. We did not need to do warfare; we were sent here to rest. God had us double, triple covered, no evil could come nigh our dwelling.

How many times however are we called to be a prayer covering for someone and we fall short of the diligence expressed by these men and women guarding the Jewel Paradise Resort? I do not know when or if ever there had been an attack on this resort, but they were prepared like it happens once a week. What a lesson for me - for us all. We know that we are in a spiritual war. The threat is real, and it is imminent. The body of Christ is under constant attack, and we are to war against the enemy for ourselves, our families, our ministries, our communities, our government and all those that God specifically put on our hearts.

I believe with all my heart that our prayer intercessors at VIP and Pastoral Staff (along with many others) keep us covered in prayer. However, one morning I was moved to attend 5am prayer at the church.

I slipped in quietly as possible in the back and fell to my knees hoping to not be seen. Somehow being the Bishop's wife always seems to alter whatever was going on before my arrival. My desire was to just quietly join in and add my prayers into the mix of whatever was occurring.

As the prayer progressed, Minister Linda, a prayer warrior for certain, begin to pray for my husband, the Bishop. She prayed from the hair follicles on his head to the nails on his toes. She named every system of his body and most if not all of his body parts. Next, she began to pray for me. I got so engrossed in the thoroughness of her prayer at some point I quit praying and just began to listen. I now know what God wanted me to know, without any doubt, was that though there are always threats and dangers lurking about, there will always be those that He has called to intercede on our behalf that will do so with thoroughness and completeness as to not leave one detail out.

Here's what I know. We never need to shift our focus from an assignment or rest that God has given to us. No matter what happens in life, stand your ground, diligently attend to your post. If we leave our assignment to run here and there chasing after the enemy, he (the devil) will continue to send fires to act as distractions from what God intends for us to do. We should be informed by developing issues around us, but we should not be distracted by them. The watchers were watching. The servers were serving. We were sent on retreat with specific instructions to rest; rest in preparation for what God wanted to do next in our lives. We saw the security, we knew there was something brewing, but God had all of that under control. If, in the times of trouble, everyone leaves their assigned post to react to the trouble, chaos will ensue, not just now but also in the future. The assignment that should have had us prepared for our futures will be stalled and incomplete.

Rufus and I were blessed to complete and thoroughly enjoy our vacation - our time of rest. Whatever threatened to occur was avoided and did not come to fruition. We came back energized and renewed, ready to hear from God and continue serving His people in excellence, at His great pleasure.

REFLECTION POINTS

"Do not be afraid of them; the LORD your God himself will fight for you."

Deuteronomy 3:22

"Have I not commanded you? Be strong and courageous. Do not be afraid; do not be discouraged, for the LORD your God will be with you wherever you go."

Joshua 1:9

1. What do these verses say to you in your present circumstance?

2. Have you been distracted from assignments you were specifically given to accommodate people or to accommodate situations unfolding before you?

3. It is crucial that you hear clearly from God and attend to what God has called you to. How do you stay informed by situations but not distracted by them?

4. How has this verse brought you peace, in potentially dangerous situations?

CHAPTER 20
TAKING GOD'S BREATH FOR GRANTED

Most people go through life for months or years, at a time, and give no thought to whether or not they will continue in the next moment, with the ability to breathe. Usually, if we get choked on a piece of rice or some other foreign food object that goes down the wrong way, we desperately gasp to clear our air passageways and we think about breathing, only for a moment. Unless we are born with or develop a problem with our respiratory system, we tend to take our next breaths for granted. "Take a deep breath and blow out your candles." or "Take a deep breath and jump in (the water)." I've said it. I've said it with a focus on the candles. I've said it with a focus on the water. And I acknowledge that too often I have failed to give proper focus or attention to the actual breath held in my lungs. In the Bible, the book of Genesis tells us that God formed us from the dust of the ground, and God breathed breath into our nostrils, and then we became living beings. There is no way around it, we simply cannot remain alive without breath in our bodies. But God has a way of getting our attention.

In January 2019, there was an announcement of a mysterious virus originating from Wuhan City, Hubei Province, China. The virus starts out with mild or common symptoms such as cough, fever or chills, but over the next few days can develop into more serious symptoms, such as difficulty breathing with other respiratory issues. By the end of 2021, after studying the virus, as it spread worldwide, the United States had over 20 million Covid-19 infections and about 350 thousand resulting deaths. We were dealing with a pandemic that literally and figuratively, took our breaths away. A pandemic is named when there is a disease that results in death, it is spread through person-to-person contact and it has impact all over the world. Many of us were caught off guard and were unprepared for the moment.

In a matter of a few short months, our world was turned upside down. There were stay at home orders issued and curfews set. Businesses, restaurants, transportation all came to a screeching halt. Churches and other non profits were ordered to close their doors. Some clergy immediately posted, 'closed until further notice signs', on their doors. Some clergy defied orders and continued meeting, despite the Executive Order. And, some, like our ministry, scrambled to assemble a team of leaders who could quickly carry out tasks to ensure we not miss a beat.

Several of our pastoral staff and leaders were already assembled at the church, for a different purpose, when the executive order for California was announced. After a brief time of planning, prayer, and, of course, worship, we all had our marching orders. We had a communication plan, and timeline, and a developed message for the congregants. Thanks to the expertise of our musician and Magnification director, Justin, and the extraordinary skill and ability of our audio visual technician, Keven, Jr., we were able to pivot to online services without missing a beat. The Mission's Department directors, Diahanna and Tara quickly assembled a list of all members and created a plan to deliver groceries and other essential items to seniors, so they would not have to leave their homes. Those that contracted the virus received 'Covid boxes' that included fresh fruit, vegetables, over-the-counter medication to relieve virus symptoms, and activity items to help with the passage of time. Families with small children received boxes that also included small toys and school supplies. Lots of prayer and love were tucked into the corners of each box. Our Administrator, Penni, and the Maturity Department ensured that the seniors also had access to technology so they would not be isolated or without the ability to sit in on the provided services. Our Board and Finance Department made sure there were multiple ways to give online. The youth department created weekly group sessions for the kids to dial in and hear an age-appropriate message and join in on a game of hangman or scavenger hunt.

Because of my love of reading, I narrated books for children and adults online to work against loneliness and boredom. There were people from my congregation and those I knew in the community that would listen each week. But over the weeks, I noticed there were also individuals joining that I had never met. The Bishop preached and taught in our living room, to me and the dropped-off equipment, just as fervently as he did standing in front of the full congregation. Though we were in a 'shutdown state, the reach of our ministry grew. We begin seeing people dial into our Facebook or YouTube channel that was signing on from Chicago, Atlanta, Tennessee, and even South Africa.

These were strange and unfamiliar times. Fear and misinformation were running rampant. Some people believed the virus was real, some thought it to be some form of government manipulation. News and official reports were frequently contradictory in nature. People hoarded food as well as nonperishable items, and drug and alcohol consumption reportedly increased. Never in our lifetime were we surrounded with news of so much death and sickness; a sickness that carried with it the possible result of more death. There was lots of hand washing and mask-wearing, yet almost everyone knew someone, personally, that had died of Covid-19. Hospitals were turning people away and encouraging stay-at-home care. Because the virus attacked the respiratory system, hospitals began running out of available ventilators. Many people died in their homes, unable to reach medical professionals with access to the needed equipment. Mortuaries were quickly reaching capacity and burials were delayed for indefinite amounts of time. Child abuse and suicides skyrocketed and many seniors were isolated in their homes. All we could do was pray and continue meeting the needs, as best as we could, to continue showing the love of Jesus, and to counter the horrors that this pandemic was bringing.

At some point, halfway through the pandemic, churches were allowed to return to in-person services, at a limited capacity, while maintaining the mask mandate. We continued our online services, but because of the size of our building, we were able to allow up to 100 in attendance at the church, while conforming to a 6-foot social distancing stipulation. One Sunday, towards the end of the Bishop's sermon, he looked particularly tired and a bit dazed or disoriented. As he finished he sat down and when it was time to leave, after service, he said he needed just a bit more time.

When the Bishop finally stood, he said he was tired and still a bit dizzy. The primary known Covid symptoms at the time were coughing, shortness of breath and loss of taste and smell. Bishop was not experiencing any of those symptoms so no one expected Covid. Later in the day, after we were home, Bishop casually mentioned that he was 'still' experiencing a feeling best described as electric shock impulses in his brain and he had slight chest pain. I told him none of that was okay, especially after he said it had been happening for a couple of days! I took him to the emergency room with explicit directions on what he was to tell them. You see, at this point if you had to go into an emergency room, you could not bring anyone with you. Bishop was known to give shallow responses that would not give the doctors a complete picture of what he was dealing with.

After remaining in the emergency room for, what seemed like an eternity, but was probably closer to four hours, he came out with instructions to schedule a Covid test the next day with his doctor. I was outdone! At this point, it seemed they were calling everything Covid. We followed up and he took the test. Because everything was backed up, it would be almost a week before he would receive results.

During the waiting period, the Bishop seemingly was quickly deteriorating. He had difficulty concentrating and lost his appetite. All he wanted to do was sleep and he frequently stared into space. He would start a sentence and then trail off. He was still dizzy. We did not have the results back yet but they needed to do something, Covid or not. I drove him to Modesto Kaiser ready to put up a fight for him to be seen. He needed a wheelchair by the time we arrived and they took him in immediately. Because of Covid, much of the triage was done outside and I could see them administering a rapid Covid test on him. Within 20 minutes the results returned positive. We learned his oxygen was compromisingly low and because Bishop has a few other health issues, Covid was wreaking havoc on his system. He was admitted into ICU.

During this time period, many people who went into ICU, and especially those that were placed on ventilators, did not come home. Our families, the entire church body and those closely connected began fasting and praying. Thank God for our Associated Pastor James that stepped up to lead and the Pastoral Staff that filled any gaps. Ministry continued but there was now a distraction, a dark cloud hanging over the congregation. A 24 hour prayer vigil was called and people stayed on a prayer line for the entire period praying, reading scripture, and singing songs of worship. After leaving Bishop at the hospital, I came home extremely exhausted. I went to bed an slept soundly until late in the morning the following day. I was in contact with his doctors who was having problems regulating his numbers. They were concerned they would lose him. The next day, I spoke to my husband via video on his iPad, but he struggled to formulate his thoughts, his breathing was labored and it took everything in him just to gather the breath to speak. He quit trying and just waved me off the connection. It was heartbreaking to hear and to watch and the experience seemed to take a lot out of me. I slept most of that day as well.

Three days after Bishop was admitted, and while he was still struggling in ICU, I was required to be on a zoom call. I had been selected as one of the twelve Independent Redistricting Commissioners for the

State of California and we had an extensive amount of training to complete. I could not seem to stay awake during the call and was having a bit of difficulty concentrating. At break, I grabbed some grapes from my refrigerator to help me stay awake. When I felt I needed a wake up boost I popped some grapes in my mouth and almost puked. The grapes were horrible and tasted defiled. I turned off my camera, spit out the grapes into a napkin and carefully examined them to see what I really put in my mouth. It was just the green grapes. It wasn't until that moment, even before a Covid test, that I knew, oh my word, I have Covid-19!

Covid was unkind to both of us. After a week in ICU, my husband came home with an oxygen tank and was still not out of the woods. I was never admitted but made frequent trips to the emergency room when my oxygen level or heart rate would drop too low. The Covid team constantly monitored my health, online and gave instructions on what I should do to attempt to raise or lower my numbers. During this time, I had difficulty talking or breathing, I developed problems with my heart, my digestive system stopped functioning and I passed out a couple of times, without warning. I had no strength to do anything and could not tell the days from nights. I was lethargic and could not hold a complete thought in my mind. Confirmed later with my husband, we both had running irrational rapid-fire thoughts in our heads. I would worry about the one side of our house that had only paper on it and wonder what to do about it. I was horrified over the red ketchup spilled on my white chair and that Rufus would be upset over the mess. Things like this and many others would run over and over nonstop in my mind. Here's the thing. None of the thoughts were factual or had any validity. I promise, all of the walls of our house were solid and none had paper. Even with the stained white chair, if this ever did happen, Rufus would perhaps attempt to clean the chair and would more than likely just buy a new one. But he would never sweat me over a chair and I have no experience of being fearful of him finding out anything. Nevertheless, when I could catch myself doing it, I would have spent long amounts of time in some nonsensical cycle of thought.

It was not this way for everyone. Matter of fact, I believe that one thing that attributed to the quick spread of Covid-19 was it's varied impact, based on the person that contracted it. Some people that contracted the virus only had minor symptoms. For these individuals, their truth and lived experience was that Covid was the same as a bad cold. Still others, were what we came to know as asymptomatic. This meant that though the person would test positive for the Covid-19 virus, they felt absolutely no symptoms. They could not believe that they were being asked to stay home and isolate. Our testimony was that Covid was vile and horrid and something no one should ever risk contracting. It was interesting that we would hear church people state that they weren't concerned about getting Covid-19 because they were 'covered' by God. Well, this was interesting because for certain we were 'covered' as well, yet God allowed us to walk through this sickness. We would engage in discussion as we felt people were open to hear. Some individuals, we just left to their own thought process.

Despite it all, Bishop and I were both clear that there is purpose in every single thing that God allows. We trust God to use us in any plan that He has. If He determines that He wants to use us to bring Him glory in our sickness, we are here for it. We knew that whether we lived or died we would win. During our extended bout with Covid, though neither of us were fearful as to whether or not we would live or die, there were others close to our hearts, that definitely had concern. In addition to the prayers and faithfulness of our church family, our natural families were interceding on our behalf, asking God to heal us and restore complete health. We are the youngest in each of our respective families. Our sisters later told us that they simply were not prepared to let either of us go.

With both of us unable to care for ourselves or attend to our affairs, God used our daughter, the one and only, Tia Lynn, to nurture and boss us back to life. Now Tia, had a husband, children, a job and a whole life to run but when I tell you that we were able to see love in action, she was masterful in the way she ensured we were well cared for. I am grateful for my son, in love, JJ, for supporting her while she took on this extra labor of love. Tia arranged for meal preparation through members of our congregation, friends, and family. We will forever be grateful for every dish prepared for us, in love. As result, every single day we had food, juice and water that we did not have to worry about preparing or searching out. She arranged for meals to be dropped off at her house, to minimize exposure to others as well as to control visitors so we could have maximum rest to aid recovery. Her daily ritual would begin with a ring of our doorbell, or a knock, (even though she's always had a key to any home we were in), and in her cheery, high-pitched, sing-songy voice, would say, "Good Morning, Mom and Dad. It's me." Every day, Tia would show up, fully masked, gloved, and covered (protected) from head to toe. Our daughter would clean and sanitize surfaces in our home, change and wash sheets, as needed, serve the pre-prepared meals, pick up previous containers, check or inquire about our health levels, make pharmacy runs, and ensure we had anything she thought we needed. Many days, I would only be vaguely aware of her presence. She would then go home, strip in her wash room shower, and redress before interacting with her family. The ritual went on for about two months. This daughter of ours was exactly what we needed; she was a huge blessing in our lives, when we needed it the most.

After a long period of time, God began to restore our health. There was a collective sigh that was felt by our families and church members. We begin to share our testimony of surviving Covid-19 and was instrumental in the community at large in dispelling some of the myths and rumors. Because of our very public lives, people heard our story and begin to think differently concerning Covid and their responses to it. The experience caused us to be aware of the preciousness of life, at a whole new level. We were gifted with new determination to serve God to the best of our ability. We recognized that life is indeed short and we gained new clarity around the phrase tomorrow is not promised. A few weeks after I returned to my social justice work, Pastor Ben was leading us through an exercise designed to help us relax and prepare to be 'in the moment'. He asked the participants on our zoom call to take a deep breath and hold it for a count of 10. As I took the breath, I had to turn off my camera because tears began to flow down my face. I was overcome with gratitude in just being able to take a deep breath. Covid only allowed quick shallow breaths, as deep ones would bring spasms of coughing. Coughing out causes you to automatically breathe in and so would start a cycle of coughing fits, that each time I was unsure I would come out of. In that moment, I recalled the time period where I could not sing aloud praises to God, because it required deep breathing from the diaphragm. After living through Covid, I realize the sweetness of the breath in my body. I took time to take another deep breath, to the count of ten. As I exhaled, I was fully aware of whose breath I was breathing. God is the breath giver and every breath taken is a precious gift from God.

REFLECTION POINTS

"Then the LORD God formed a man from the dust of the ground and breathed into his nostrils the breath of life, and the man became a living being."

Genesis 2:7 NIV

1. Gratitude for the hidden things: In addition to the precious gift of breath, list other things that you can be grateful to God for. How many of these things do you typically take for granted?

2. Acts of kindness: You may never be called upon to arrange daily meals for someone outside of your household. However, what are some things you can do to show love, especially for those who may never know what you've done?

CHAPTER 21
PEACE MUST BE CHOSEN

Very often, especially when things are good, I just don't want the thing to end. I want one or two more scenes to a good movie. I desire just a few more chapters in an exciting novel. Just one more scoop of that hard-to-find Rocky Road ice cream with walnuts ... You get the picture. Conclusion - the end of an event or program; the cessation of something that had been on-going; the finale or wrap-up of a story. Sometimes, a conclusion shows up a lot sooner than when we anticipated it would.

Recently, my husband and I was required to travel to southern California to conclude the life affairs of our first born child. At 42 years of age, our only son 'concluded' his time here on this earth and crossed over into life eternal. No one predicted, felt it, or saw it coming. We were shocked, devastated, and for a while, in denial and in total disbelief. For sure, this felt like a premature conclusion; a life ended too soon. Many of you may have lost children and can relate to the level of pain and anguish we were experiencing. At some point after the news of his passing, and after the wailing, beyond the involuntary heaves, and silent tears, came the unbearable weight of raw grief.

We are familiar with books that reveal how to recognize the stages of grief using five steps, seven steps, eight steps or twelve. It occurred to me, early on, that the grief that was threatening to suffocate me and overtake my life could not be carried one step, let alone twelve. I want to talk about, not the steps of grief so much as, I want to talk about grief. I had previous and recent experience with grief and from my perspective, grief is a spirit that, if you allow it, will totally consume any and everything that was ever good in your life. Grief has a way of erupting out of the bowels of your being and overtaking every rational thought in your head. The deep, deep sadness, the void and the felt brokenness, all amplifying the loss of something you valued and that you held dear. As I desperately tried to process and catch up with what God had already decided for our lives, at some point, I became aware of a deceptive lure, to wholly give in to the abyss that the fulness of grief had to offer. Anguish and despair stood with their arms wide open, calling out for me to fully embrace all they had to offer.

During this state of being, where I could barely process a rational thought, the devil worked overtime to bring up old memories that he wanted me to dwell on. In particular, years later, years after I chose to forgive, the enemy reminded me that the very drug introduced to my son, by a church member, seeking to exact revenge on my husband, was the same drug that ended his life. Anguish, devastation, and yes, it was there, anger. To make matters worse there was no focal point for the anger because, the person responsible for this introduction was no longer alive. This truth and fact did not help. The devil offered, the problem was 'church people'. In grief, it is hard to hold on to rational thoughts. I had to quickly shut down that line of thinking, rebuke the enemy and once again forgive the person for the hurt and harm they caused.

The news of Jbar's death travelled quickly and my family, church family and a host of my son's friends began reaching out to us in love. Initially, I had zero capacity to hold, comfort, care, or respond to anyone about anything. The sadness was palpable and controlled my every thought. Eventually, I began to sparingly respond to the many, many individuals that were also shocked and saddened by the news. The

Spirit of God started highlighting and calling attention to my responses. Rather than the customary, "fine" in response to how I was doing, I sifted through my emotions for just the right words to describe my state of being. In searching for the truest sense of what I felt - despair, hurt, brokenness, devastation, and extreme sadness, seemed to scream out louder than anything else. Once again, I sensed the Spirit's stirring. Each time that I responded, naming the feelings that took center stage in my mind, I could sense God's Spirit grieving. At first, I thought it was God's Spirit grieving with me, then I began to see, no, God's Spirit was grieving for me.

I would type, "I am devastated" or "My heart is so broken" and there would be the ever so faint whisper, "You don't have to be." And with every 'true' expression of what was real, so real to me - anguish, despair, unbelievable sorrow, suffocating pain, there was awareness of a counter that offered hope, healing and renewal. What in the world was going on? My extraordinarily gifted and talented son was less than two weeks deceased, of course I would feel all of those things. I was not pretending to be in anguish, I was! I did not desire to be devastated, I was devastated and could not imagine ever being okay, without my son alive and well.

Why would I chose to respond in a manner that was not true? Scriptures began coming to me that promised peace in times of despair, joy for sorrow, and beauty for ashes. There was scripture that promised that God was a present help in times of despair and a mender of broken hearts. Yes, I know that God is a mender of broken hearts, but did I want Him to mend my heart, and so soon? This is my child, my first born, my only son and this pain is mines to carry. The pain and grief felt right - there was that deceptive lure again. It was palpable enough to hold on to when I could no longer hold on to my boy. And, if I let it go, what would I have?

I am, we are, used to holding on to pain, suffering, disappointment, or grief, as some sort of consolation prize, for long periods of time, even years. We nurture it, coddle it and after we have paid the hefty price for claiming ownership for so long and after it has robbed us of years of what should have been gratifying, new lived experiences and joys, we are beaten down enough, we have finally lost enough, to decide to release our tight grip, on this that never was a prize. Grief is a valid, God-given emotion but the enemy is constantly seeking to pervert what God has allowed. There was a sinister plot behind the call to continue my downward-spiral into the darkness.

The clarity of the battle that I was dealing with and what was at stake, started to crystalize in my mind. This was not about whether or not the grief was real, it was real. Grief has the power to take control of your thoughts, your desire to get up or even your desire to live. This was more about, would I trust God to 'right-size' the grief and to appropriately couple it with the truth of who God is, with His power and with His ability. Psalm 73:26 tells me that my heart and my strength may fail but God is the strength of my heart and mines forever.

The Spirit of God was grieving or saddened because each time I partnered with the enemy, even though I was stating a truth, I was speaking and solidifying what the enemy wanted for my life - brokenness and devastation. Just gaining clarity on what I was doing and in knowing that I never want to willingly partner with the devil, I began to get my first fresh breaths since that fateful call relaying Jbar's death. I had to start speaking the truth that was written in God's Word. I forgive because I stand in need of forgiveness. I have peace because God is a peace speaker. Though I don't feel I can make it through this, I can do all things through Christ Jesus who gives me strength. God's Word stands greater and stronger than any felt emotion. We hear time heals all things, but the truth in that statement is that God, the Creator of time, heals all things and He stands outside of time and can heal in an instant.

People, all over the world, were interceding on our behalf, praying for peace, strength and comfort, during this difficult time of loss. God is a prayer-answering God. What I learned is that though God stands ready to provide peace, I had to choose peace. God wants us to feel His love and rest in His strength but we have to choose to accept and trust His love and rely on His power and strength. With this awareness and leading of the Holy Spirit, I fought to choose the promises of Jesus. This was not a casual or passive decision. I had to fight to hold fast to every scripture I knew and allow God to bathe me in Hs love, drown out the voice and lies of the enemy, and then desperately press my way up and out from the pits of despair.

The ending or conclusion, that the devil had for me, was that he would be able to use this tragic loss to have me slip into unforgiveness and bitterness. He wanted to mute my praise and minimize my faith in God. But, sometimes you get that desired next chapter, the one that actually changes the whole story. I am so glad that this story didn't end in the direction it was heading. God did give me His promised peace. Through the whole process, God was right there giving us the strength we needed, day by day. There are still hidden land mines that I occasionally stumble upon. These land mines come in the form of certain phrases, songs, or particular memories. Land mines - once in conversation, totally unrelated to loss, I was recalling an event from my past and mentioned something to do with my kids. Land mine, with a fresh flow of tears. I realized that I no longer have kids, as in two. I now only have a child, as in one. Who knew this simple realization would expose open a wound and bring fresh pain? These unexpected moments may bring feelings of sadness or longing and they may bring a flood of fresh tears, However, in choosing God's peace, I didn't have to wait months or years for that debilitating grief to slowly subside. I experienced the power of God first-hand. I discovered that God really is a present help in the times of trouble.

REFLECTION POINTS

"God is our refuge and strength [mighty and impenetrable], A very present and well-proved help in trouble."
Psalms 46:1 AMP

"I am leaving you with a gift—peace of mind and heart. And the peace I give is a gift the world cannot give. So don't be troubled or afraid."
Psalms 14:27 NLT

1. What pain from your past are you struggling with? Are you ready to allow the God of peace to be a present help for you?

_____

_____

_____

_____

2. How can you allow the loss to draw you closer to God?

_____

_____

_____

CHAPTER 22
WHAT WE DO WITH IT?

"Mrs. Turner, what do we do with it?" In that moment, a profound lesson was etched into my consciousness. I had never been so keenly made aware of how another individual can love you so completely that they put their total trust in you. The lesson has resonated and remained with me for more than 20 years now. Mrs. Turner, what do we do with it? This question has returned to me more times than I would have ever imagined.

I was teaching a small group of children, ten or so, of various ages during a bible study held in my home. The lesson was on being grateful and learning to say thank you, to God and others. I had just handed out various objects to the children consisting of note pads, pencils, stickers, and other such trinkets. When it was apparent that I was going to run out, I was prompted by the Holy Spirit to give, with the same excitement and generosity, a couple of popsicle sticks. Yes, I gave out the sticks completely void of the popsicle or any such thing.

Because of the lesson, each recipient accepted their gift and said thank you. One of the recipients of the plain, wooden 'prize' was one of the youngest in attendance. I will never, ever forget the look on her face when she accepted the stick. Somewhat shy, but with bright eyes and a huge smile, Mariah said, "Thank You!" I went on with the lesson pretending to be totally oblivious to the fact that a couple of the children received sticks.

After about five minutes had passed, as all of the other children were distracted by their trinkets and treasures, I heard Mariah say, "Mrs. Turner, what do we do with it?" As I turned to look at her my heart melted. With the same smile and only a hint of confusion, she held out the stick towards me as she waited patiently for the answer. Her question and facial expression confirmed the fact that she wasn't clear on how this was a gift at all. But her actions, vocal inflections, and the look of expectancy on her face said, "I do not quite understand or get the point, but I love and trust you so much that I know it must be just me; there has got to be some wonderful thing that is going to come out of this stick!"

Oh, that we can learn to come to God, like Mariah, with childlike wonder even when we do not understand. Not with a demanding why that is veiled in accusations of failure or cruelty. But in asking questions while straining to hold on to the fact that all I know of You is that You are good and kind. You are a loving God that always has my best interest at heart. What do I do with this God? There has to be something wonderful in it. Is it something that will grow me up? Is it something that will weed some things out? Is it something that will draw me closer to You? What do I do with this? To me 'this' looks broken or used, or no good, or useless. It looks like everyone else has received their desires and dreams. Everyone else has it better than me. They have received treasures that sparkle and shine. They have received obvious tools that can be used to create other things. What You have given me has no apparent value or worth.

Rather than take this approach, when we feel we've gotten, 'the short end of a stick' or a raw deal, we often throw our own personal version of a tantrum and declare God to be an unfit caregiver.

Our actions state, God, though you have covered and upheld me so many other times, I cannot trust you now - not for this. I really only trust You when I can see what you are doing, when I know what You are up to AND when I agree with Your shared plan of action! I don't actually trust You to have my best interest at heart. And about this thing that You currently have me facing … I am at a loss here, God. This one I cannot pretend to get. What do I do with this? You actually chose this, for me?

It's in these moments that the Word should wake up in us. In the times when we didn't get the check in the mail, when the spouse didn't return, when the house went into foreclosure, when the child did die… You know, when the thing you were believing God for, had a different outcome than what you were believing God for. In these moments, can we still respond with an undaunted smile and a light in our eyes, and ask our loving Father, "Father God, what we do with it?"

How proud I was of Mariah. I knew how to say thank you and be grateful for a good gift. But Mariah taught me how to look beyond the perceived value of the gift and to see the value and richness in the gift-giver. Mariah loved and trusted me enough that even if she did not understand the gift, she emphatically knew, fighting against any trace of doubt, that if Mrs. Turner gave it to her, it was just what she needed! She taught me a lesson of gratitude and trust that day that I have never forgotten. I hear Paul in God's word saying to be thankful in all circumstances, "for this is God's will for you who belong to Christ." I emphatically trust God. He has only good thoughts towards me. Every good and perfect gift comes from Him. As long as I belong to Christ, He has ordained every circumstance in my life, and regardless of whether or not I understand the thing that has occurred, whether it is God sent, or God allowed, I am grateful for it, even when I don't know what to do with it.

REFLECTION POINTS

"In everything give thanks; for this is God's will for you in Christ Jesus."

1 Thessalonians 5:18

1. Gratitude: Are you only thankful for good gifts from God? What would it look like for you to be thankful for an undesired outcome?

2. What does it look like for you to always trust God, as a good Father that cares deeply for you?

SLEEPING WITH THE BISHOP

I believe that God masterfully cloaks our future. We may catch glimpses of His purpose for our lives now and then, but I wholeheartedly believe that God knows we cannot handle the fullness of His plans, until His appointed timing through bit-by-bit revelation. I had not an inkling, back in September of 1978 of what all my, "I do" entailed. That covenant made, between me, the (now) Bishop, and God included print that was written so fine, that only time could magnify and bring the words to light. I was saying I do to a quiet, young church boy that played the piano for the choir. I said yes to a Bank of America research technician that dressed in a way that would never have him pegged to be a preacher or pastor.

Two children, a dog, job changes, and a couple of houses later, God called and ordained my husband to plant, build, and lead a ministry. Though this was never named in our goals and discussions concerning our future together, the call into ministry, for my husband, was not farfetched or too big of a surprise. He was practically born during a church service, according to his mother. My husband received Christ at 9 years of age and embraced every aspect of Christianity and the strict Apostolic faith that we grew up in. As a teen, he loved attending Sunday school, bible study, revivals, and prayer meetings.

TRENA TURNER

My husband grew up in the church. I grew up around the church. I did not like bible study or Sunday school, or prayer meetings or revivals. Sunday service was fun because there were a good number of other kids and we would tease the older people for the way they worshipped God and we would sometimes sneak to the corner store, during church. There was an older man that would stand out front and give the kids candy or walnuts and an older lady that would sell peanuts. A couple of times a year, if you were part of the youth group, you got to go on snow trips or to a dinner in the city (SF). For me, this made church tolerable.

Eventually, thank God, I accepted Christ and received the gift of the Holy Spirit. Beyond that being life-changing for me, it was, in retrospect, crucial that I accepted Christ as my own because I am certain the church boy would never have proposed to me if I had remained a non-Christian. I think it took me longer to decide if I wanted to be 'saved' because I was very opinionated, about everything. Things needed to make sense - to me. I was not a follower of the crowds or a do-it-because-I said type girl. I had a thought about everything and I was not afraid to share my thoughts, invited, or not. I would have never seen myself as a pastor's wife. I would have never seen myself as a bishop's wife. Even when my husband was first called to pastor, people, right away, wanted to tell me how I would have to be or act. I quickly let them know that I believed God knew exactly who I was and who I was not. I hadn't made a practice of being someone else up to that point and I would not start then.

I had the opportunity to study about the wonder of a seed, for a sermon I was blessed to share. Whether a seed will eventually be an apple tree or a majestic oak, as a seed, it already has everything in it that it needs, to be what it will become. External sources - water, sunlight, soil, all have bearing on its growth but the identification of what it is and what it is capable of has already been predetermined by the Creator. When God created my husband, even before his awareness of his call into ministry, God also selected and hand-crafted me to serve at His side. No one else could have done it as I can. I was built for this. When

God created me, he placed in me all that I would need to be identified as who I am. God placed the right amount of boldness, patience, wonder, and love for His people. Any character flaws that I and others saw in me, God declared them to be attributes that He could use.

Years later, with full knowledge of the ups and downs, hurts and pains, I still 'do'. I am not angry with God over one moment of this life, in all of its twists and turns. Sleeping with the Bishop, sharing life from this perspective, has been an awesome privilege and an honor, and one that I would not change for the world.

> *"Before I formed thee in the belly I knew thee; and before thou camest forth out of the womb I sanctified thee, and I ordained thee a prophet unto the nations."*
>
> Jeremiah 1:5 KJV